CHAMELEONS

Chris Mattison and Nick Garbutt

FIREFLY BOOKS

A Firefly Book

Published by Firefly Books Ltd. 2012

First printing

Publisher Cataloging-in-Publication
Data (U.S.)

Mattison, Chris.
Chameleons / Chris
Mattison and Nick Garbutt.
[112] p. : col. photos. ; cm.
Includes bibliographical references and index.
Summary: Guide to chameleon biology and natural
history, explaining why they look as they do and why
they vary in size, shape and color; includes details of
where to see chameleons in the wild and how to look
after them in the home.
ISBN-13: 978-1-77085-121-4
1. Chameleons. I. Garbutt, Nick. II. Title.
597.956 dc23   QL666.L23M388 2012

Library and Archives Canada Cataloguing in Publication

Mattison, Christopher
Chameleons / Chris Mattison & Nick Garbutt. — 1st ed.
Includes index.
ISBN 978-1-77085-121-4
1. Chameleons. 2. Chameleons—Pictorial works. I. Garbutt, Nick II. Title.
QL666.L23M37 2012   597.95'6   C2012-900773-0

Published in the United States by
Firefly Books (U.S.) Inc.
P.O. Box 1338, Ellicott Station
Buffalo, New York 14205

Published in Canada by
Firefly Books Ltd.
66 Leek Crescent
Richmond Hill, Ontario L4B 1H1

Designed by Mercer Design, London
Reproduction and printing by C&C Offset Printing Co., Ltd. China

First published by the
Natural History Museum
Cromwell Road
London SW7 5BD

Contents

Introduction

OF ALL THE LIZARDS, THE CHAMELEONS are the most charismatic. Although they are objects of fear and superstition in some of the places where they live, to Western eyes they are amusing curiosities even among the many people who otherwise dislike reptiles. They have made their way into the English language as a metaphor for fickle or changeable behaviour and they have lent their name to organisations that want to advertise the adaptability of their services and products.

For visitors to Madagascar they are one of the 'must see' animals. Along with other groups of unique animals from that remarkable island, and in parts of East Africa, children bring chameleons, clinging to sticks, to show tourists in the hope of earning a small reward. Chameleons are, of course, harmless, although a few can give a painful bite if they are handled roughly. But it is their unique appearance that makes them so remarkable. This is the result of the way in which they have adapted to their environment. Their body shape and their ability to change colour keep them hidden from predators. Their pincer-like feet and prehensile tails turn them into them expert climbers, while their independently swivelling eyes and projectile tongues help them to find and capture food. The chameleon is the Swiss Army knife of the reptile world.

Although most chameleons follow the same basic plan, they vary in size, shape and colour. The smallest species are shorter than a matchstick and eat mites, springtails and other barely-visible creatures that live on the forest floor, whereas the largest ones are ferocious hunters that think nothing of crunching their way through large, heavily-armoured beetles, small lizards and even mice. Many species have crests, horns and bony helmet-like structures on their heads, giving them a prehistoric appearance. And they live in such amazing places; from the green and soggy rain forests of eastern Madagascar to the arid Namib Desert, one of the driest places on Earth. Coming across a chameleon in its own environment is always an exciting event.

Like reptiles in many parts of the world, chameleons are under pressure from human activities, most notably land clearance and development. At the same time as new species are being discovered (four were named while this book was in preparation, for instance) others are being pushed towards extinction. We hope that this brief account of chameleons will stimulate interest and answer some of the questions about them. Increasing our knowledge and appreciation of them is the first step towards preserving them, their habitats, and the other plants and animals that live alongside them.

ABOUT THE AUTHORS

CHRIS MATTISON Graduating with an honours degree in zoology from the University of Sheffield, Chris went on to specialise in the natural history of reptiles and amphibians. He is an award-winning photographer and has made field trips to many parts of the world, including visits to North, Central and South America, southern Africa, East Africa, Southeast Asia and Madagascar, to study and photograph reptiles and amphibians in the field.

He has lectured to audiences in the United Kingdom, Sweden, Finland, Holland and the United States on the natural history of reptiles and amphibians, their responsible care in captivity, and on nature photography. Since 1982, has written over 20 books, including *Frogs and Toads*, *Snake* and *The Encycopedia of Snakes*, as well as many magazine articles on these topics.

NICK GARBUTT An award winning photographer and critically acclaimed author, Nick has a particular interest in islands and rainforests and is best known for his work on Madagascar and Borneo. He has had a lifelong fascination for reptiles, and on Madagascar has observed a significant proportion of the islands' chameleons as well as other species on the African mainland. As well as *Chameleons* his other books include: *100 Animals to See Before They Die*, *Mammals of Madagascar: A Complete Guide*, *Wild Borneo* and *Madagascar Wildlife: A Visitor's Guide*.

CHAPTER 1

Evolution and classification

CHAMELEONS ARE THE SOLE MEMBERS of the family Chamaeleonidae. They are among the most recognisable of lizards, due to a unique combination of features: five toes that are fused into a pair of opposable pincer-like structures; a tongue that they can shoot out to a great length; eyes that rotate independently of each other; and non-overlapping, stud-like scales. These features separate them from all other lizards. Other characteristics, common to most but not all species, include a prehensile tail; a laterally flattened, leaf-like shape; randomly scattered large scales interspersed among smaller, evenly sized ones; bony ridges on their heads; and crests of enlarged tooth-shaped scales running down the centre of their backs and, in some species, along the ventral midline as well. A number of species have additional horns or flaps on their snouts. Many of these features are adaptations to a diurnal, arboreal and insectivorous lifestyle.

OPPOSITE A male crested chameleon, *Trioceros cristatus*, shows the high dorsal crest for which this species is named, and intense breeding coloration. It comes from West Africa, where it lives in low shrubs and bushes.

BELOW All chameleons, like this flap-necked chameleon, *Chamaeleo dilepis*, share a distinctive and recognisable body plan. They are laterally compressed, have fused toes, a prehensile tail and independently swivelling eyes.

Those species which are most arboreal are predominantly green in colour whereas species that live on the ground or in low vegetation are often brown, and are commonly referred to as 'leaf chameleons'. Many species, especially the larger, showy ones, can change colour and pattern rapidly in response to their mood: chameleons are highly visual lizards and their displays are often spectacular, although their ability to change colour to match their background is greatly exaggerated. (The so-called American 'chameleons' belonging to the genus *Anolis* share with the true chameleons the ability to change colour, though not to such a great extent, but do not possess any of the other adaptations mentioned above. They are members of a different family, the Polychrotidae, more closely allied to the iguanas.)

OPPOSITE The American 'chameleons' actually belong to a different family, but are so-called because they have a limited ability to change their colour. This is the green anole, *Anolis carolinensis*, a common species throughout the southeastern states of North America.

ORIGINS OF THE CHAMELEONS

The chameleons are among the oldest families of lizards, coming from an ancestral line that may go back over 100 million years. Their closest relatives are the agamids, Agamidae, members of which include the dragon lizards of Southeast Asia and Australia and numerous small rock and tree-dwelling species from Africa. The oldest fossil clearly recognisable as a chameleon, *Chamaeleo caroliquarti*, dates from 26 million years ago and was found in Europe.

Chameleons belong to the most primitive group of lizards, known as iguanians. All the members of this group are diurnal lizards with good eyesight but a poor sense of smell. Another of their characteristics is their rounded tongues, as opposed to the forked or notched tongues of most other families of lizards. Whereas the other members of this group have short, blunt tongues, chameleons' tongues are anything but short and they use them in a unique way, turning their tips into missiles that can be shot out over long distances and with great accuracy. Because they are diurnal hunters, chameleons need to be masters of disguise if they are to successfully stalk or ambush their prey while avoiding predators.

Since branching off from the early iguanians stock, other specialisations appeared that have helped chameleons to thrive and survive, and it is this seemingly strange combination of adaptations that characterise them. Having arrived, so to speak, chameleons soon evolved into different forms, allowing them to move into different ecological niches. The main division is between the dwarf forms, sometimes known as leaf chameleons, which are brown in colour and dwell on forest floors and in low vegetation, and the more typical larger and more colourful forms that best fit in with our mental picture of what chameleons ought to be. This division is reflected in the separation of the Chamaeleonidae into two subfamilies (although not everyone accepts this arrangement). The Brookesiinae contains 48 mostly small, drab-coloured species in three genera (*Brookesia, Rhampholeon* and *Rieppeleon*) from Madagascar and parts of Central and East Africa. This grouping may prove to be based on superficial characteristics. Some scientists believe that the African and Malagasy species evolved independently of each other and their similarities are due

BELOW The dabb lizards, or mastigures, are members of the Agamidae and therefore fairly close relatives of the chameleons, although this is not immediately obvious from their general appearance. This is the Saharan dabb lizard, *Uromastyx geyri*, from North Africa.

BELOW The chameleon family divides neatly into two major groups. Considered more primitive are the leaf chameleons, subfamily Brookesiinae, which are far less arboreal and live mainly on the forest floor in leaf litter. This species is *Brookesia superciliaris* from Madagascar.

to convergent evolution. The remaining 144 species, divided into seven genera, comprise the subfamily Chamaeleoninae.

Recent research indicates that the genus *Brookesia* is the most primitive, followed by members of *Rhampholeon*, and that these are the ancestors of all other chameleons. Since *Brookesia* live in Madagascar, whereas *Rhampholeon* are African, the question arises of how these early chameleons came to be found on both landmasses. Early studies proposed that the chameleons had already evolved when Madagascar broke away from the African mainland, so that a single stock became separated into two. More recent research, however, indicates that Madagascar may have become isolated about 165 million years ago, long before chameleons had appeared, which leads to the alternative theory that chameleons spread to Africa by 'rafting', possibly on more than one occasion. A third theory is that, although Madagascar became separated from Africa early on, there were land bridges present across the Mozambique Channel at various times, allowing several waves of colonisation by chameleons. Having arrived in Africa, by whatever means, chameleons then spread from there into southern Europe, the Middle East and South Asia.

FAMILY: CHAMAELEONIDAE

SUBFAMILY: BROOKESIINAE (leaf chameleons)

Brookesia	31 species	Madagascar
Rhampholeon	14 species	Africa
Rieppeleon	3 species	Africa

SUBFAMILY: CHAMAELEONINAE ('true' chameleons)

Bradypodion	17 species	Africa
Calumma	32 species	Madagascar
Chamaeleo	17 species	Africa, Europe, Middle East and Asia
Furcifer	20 species	Madagascar
Kinyongia	17 species	Africa
Nadzikambia	2 species	Africa
Trioceros	39 species	Africa

Totals: 192 species, 10 genera, 2 subfamilies, 1 family

BELOW A short-horned chameleon, *Calumma brevicorne*, a typical member of the subfamily Chamaeleoninae, in its habitat. This species is highly arboreal although it may move to lower branches so that it can catch ground-dwelling insects such as grasshoppers, and females have to descend to the ground to lay their eggs.

DISTRIBUTION AND HABITAT

Taking the family as a whole, almost half the species of chameleons, and three of the ten genera, occur on Madagascar. Most of the remaining species live on the African mainland, with just two (*Chamaeleo chamaeleon* and *C. africanus*) in Europe, including some Mediterranean islands; two (*C. calyptratus* and *C. arabicus*) on the Arabian Peninsula; one (*C. monachus*) on Socotra in the Indian Ocean; and one (*C. zeylanicus*) in India and Sri Lanka. *C. africanus*, which occurs in Greece and Malta, and *C. chamaeleon*, from Spain and Portugal, were probably introduced there hundreds of years ago. Two species, *Furcifer cephalolepis* and *F. polleni*, are endemic to the Comoros Islands, which lie between Madagascar and East Africa. The panther chameleon, *F. pardalis*, has been introduced to Réunion and Mauritius in the Indian Ocean. A form of Jackson's chameleon, *Trioceros jacksonii xantholophus*, was introduced to Hawaii in the early 1970s, where it has successfully established itself, and, more recently, the Yemeni species, *C. calyptratus*, has been introduced into Hawaii and Florida; these two are therefore the only true chameleons living free in the New World.

Chameleons are predominantly arboreal lizards, and their adaptations – leaf-like shape, greenish coloration, modified feet and prehensile tail – are ideally suited to this habitat. As a result, at least two-thirds of the species live in forests, which may be extensive rainforests such as those in West Africa and eastern Madagascar, deciduous forests in East Africa and western and southern Madagascar, or small, isolated relic forests such as those surrounded by grasslands in East and South Africa. Even the small species belonging to the genera *Rhampholeon* and *Brookesia*, though not arboreal in the same way as most of the larger species, depend on the understorey of the forest floor, and leaf-litter, in which to hide and feed. Most of them also climb into low vegetation at night to sleep.

RIGHT Pristine rainforest in Eastern Madagascar, home to many endemic arboreal and leaf litter-dwelling species of chameleons.

LEFT A handful of species from the drier regions of Madagascar have adapted to semi-degraded and even urban environments. Oustalet's chameleon, *Furcifer oustaleti,* can even be found living in parks and large gardens in the capital city Antananarivo.

The majority of the Malagasy species occur in tropical rainforests or tropical deciduous forests, where they live in large and small trees and shrubs. Species that come from the drier regions, mainly in the west and south of the island, tend to be mostly brown in colour, as opposed to the predominantly green species in the humid east. There are plenty of exceptions to this broad generalisation, however, depending on the exact microhabitat of the species concerned. Chameleons exploit many ecological niches on the island, leading to a great diversity in size (the largest and smallest both live here), shape and behaviour, and there are species that live in tall trees, others that prefer shrubs and grasses, and some that live among the leaf-litter. A few species, notably Oustalet's chameleon, *Furcifer oustaleti,* and the jewelled chameleon, *F. lateralis,* adapt well to disturbed habitats and occur in large numbers in parks and gardens. Chameleons are very common on Madagascar and a single area may be occupied by half a dozen or more common species as well as a similar number of less conspicuous ones.

RIGHT Fynbos, consisting of fine-leaved shrubs, succulent plants and, in places, *Protea* bushes, is a specialised habitat favoured by some South African species of *Bradypodion*.

ABOVE The wide-ranging flap-necked chameleon, *Chamaeleo dilepis*, occurs in a many different habitats but is one of the few species that can be found in isolated trees and groups of trees, such as the yellow-barked acacias, *Acacia xanthophloea*, seen here in East Africa.

On the African mainland the distribution of species is more complicated. Many species live in small pockets of forests in mountains or foothills, surrounded by a vast ocean of seasonally dry grasslands, and there is less overlap of species. The various mountain ranges within the Eastern Arc Mountains in Tanzania are particularly rich in species and there may yet be some still awaiting discovery there. In South Africa, several of the many dwarf chameleons, *Bradypodion* species, live in small patches of relic forests left over from a time when they were found more or less continuously across the region. As climate change led to the fragmentation and shrinking of the forests, isolated colonies of chameleons became stranded and evolved into many different forms. Others live among the fine-leaved heath vegetation known as 'fynbos' and yet others live in grasslands. At the last count there were 17 species, three of them named since 2006, with more waiting to be formally described; many have tiny ranges and there is no gene flow between them and neighbouring species. Similarly, some of the larger species, such as Jackson's chameleon, *Trioceros jacksonii*, are montane lizards that are restricted to various isolated mountain ranges (in East Africa in the case of this species). Not all chameleons are so specific when it comes to altitude. For example, the large Meller's chameleon, *T. melleri*, occurs from sea level in Tanzania to 1,500 m (4,921 ft) in Malawi.

Of the species that have adapted to non-forested habitats, many live in scrub and open woodland within grasslands. Species such as the very widespread flap-necked chameleon, *Chamaeleo dilepis*, whose range covers nearly the entire African mainland south of the Sahara, occur in low acacia bushes and tall, isolated trees. In this species, which has probably been more widely studied than other chameleons, researchers found that during the dry season males tend to be brown and prefer low, dry shrubs in which to live, whereas females were more likely to be green and living in green shrubs. In the spring (November in the southern parts of its range) males are often seen on the ground, crossing roads and tracks, possibly in search of mates, but later in the season more females are found on the ground, presumably looking for places to lay their eggs. The same pattern may be true of other species, but none are well-enough studied for this to be confirmed.

The Namaqua chameleon, *Chamaeleo namaquensis*, is a special case, living as it does in the Namib Desert. This species has almost abandoned the use of its modified feet and prehensile tail, developed over millions of generations for climbing. It retains all the physical characteristics of an arboreal lifestyle but its tail is shorter, its legs are longer, and its toes are broader, so that its feet are more like pads than those of other species. It varies from pale buff with darker spots to almost black in colour and, like other species of *Chamaeleo*, it is capable of rapid colour change in response to light, warmth and mood. It feeds almost exclusively on the fog-gathering tenebrionid beetles and their larvae that share its seemingly inhospitable environment.

BELOW The Namib Desert is one of the harshest environments on earth, yet one species, the Namaqua chameleon *Chamaeleo namaquensis*, has abandoned a life in the trees and adapted to this inhospitable environment. Despite this, it retains all the fundamental hallmarks of its ancestral arboreal past.

ABOVE The veiled chameleon, *Chamaeleo calyptratus*, from Yemen, is a very adaptable species, occurring on dry, shrubby plateaus, in humid valleys and hillsides. Under extremely dry conditions they will eat leaves to obtain water.

The two species from the Arabian Peninsula, the veiled chameleon, *Chamaeleo calyptratus*, and the Arabian chameleon, *C. arabicus*, are adaptable arboreal species from the border regions of Yemen and Saudi Arabia. Their habitat includes dry mountainsides as well as more humid valleys and forests and they apparently live in low shrubs and scrub as well as trees. The veiled chameleon has great tolerance of temperature and humidity: its adaptability makes it one of the few chameleons that is relatively easy to keep and breed in captivity. The Mediterranean chameleon, *C. chamaeleon*, has similarly adapted to drier conditions and is found in bushes in gardens, orchards, plantations, olive groves and vineyards. This species occurs in

scattered colonies in southern Europe, several Mediterranean islands and parts of Turkey and North Africa, and it may very well have been introduced to some of these places. The Socotra chameleon, *C. monachus*, is endemic to Socotra Island, lying about 350 km (about 210 miles) off the Yemeni coast, and home to many unusual, drought-adapted, trees and plants. Unfortunately, almost nothing is known about the ecology of this species. Finally, the Indian chameleon, *C. zeylanicus*, has a wider range than either its English or scientific names would suggest as it is found in Sri Lanka, where it was first discovered, but also in much of India and parts of Pakistan. It is a typical forest species.

ABOVE The rare Indian, or Sri Lankan chameleon, *C. zeylanicus*, is a forest species but much of its natural history is otherwise unknown.

CHAPTER 2

Size and shape, colour and markings

ALL CHAMELEONS CONFORM TO A FAIRLY conservative appearance, but the 192 species are all distinct from each other in size, shape, colour or pattern, or some combination of these features. This has not happened by chance: each species has been shaped by the process of natural selection over many generations. Differences that may seem trivial to a human observer may be important factors when it comes to survival in the natural world.

SIZE

Chameleons vary in size from a few centimetres to a little over half a metre. The smallest species, and probably the world's smallest lizard, is the recently discovered *Brookesia micra*, from the forests of Madagascar, which has a maximum size of just 30 mm (1¼ in) and measures about 15 mm when it hatches from an egg that is little bigger than a grain of rice. Before this species was reported in 2012, a closely-related species, *Brookesia minima*, held this record. The largest species is Parson's chameleon, *Calumma parsonii*, also from Madagascar, which can grow to

OPPOSITE The largest of all species is the Parson's chameleon, *Calumma parsonii*, which is widespread in the eastern rainforests of Madagascar and prefers to inhabit the canopy, especially when adult. Its markings are quite variable and some authorities recognise sub-species divisions. This individual belongs to the 'cristata' group from Ranomafana National Park in the southeast.

LEFT The pygmy leaf chameleon, *Brookesia minima*, from northern Madagascar, is not only one of the world's smallest chameleons but is also among the most diminutive of all reptiles.

RIGHT Only fractionally smaller than Parson's chameleon, Oustalet's chameleon, *Furcifer oustaleti*, is a widespread species from the drier parts of Madagascar.

RIGHT Only fractionally smaller than Parson's chameleon, Oustalet's chameleon, *Furcifer oustaleti*, is a widespread species from the drier parts of Madagascar.

69.5 cm (27 in), closely followed by Oustalet's chameleon, *Furcifer oustaleti*, which grows to 68.5 cm (a shade under 27 in). The latter species tends to be more slender, however, and very large specimens are uncommon – most are significantly smaller than the maximum. The largest mainland species is Meller's chameleon, *Trioceros melleri*, which sometimes exceeds 60 cm (24 in) in total length.

BODY SHAPE

Almost all chameleons have laterally compressed bodies: that is, they are flattened from side to side. This enables them to warm up quickly by presenting a large surface to the sun (like a solar panel) and also helps them to blend in among leaves, which are roughly the same shape. Even species that have adapted to a more terrestrial lifestyle, such as the leaf chameleons, usually retain this body shape, although some species, such as the diminutive *Brookesia minima*, have a more cylindrical cross-section, while a small number of species, notably *B. decaryi* and *B. perarmata*, are wide-bodied.

RIGHT The Antsingy leaf chameleon, *Brookesia perarmata*, has a wider, more flattened, body than most other species and also has an unusual arrangement of scales on its flanks.

SCALES

Chameleons' scales are small, irregular and not overlapping like those of most other lizards. Instead, they are granular or tubercular, sometimes uniform but more often with scales of various sizes arranged more or less randomly. Larger, stud-like scales may be interspersed among these smaller scales. This is a very characteristic feature of some *Trioceros* species, such as *T. hoehnelii*, and also among the South African dwarf chameleons, *Bradypodion*. These may be arranged in irregular rows along the chameleon's flanks, as in the Cape dwarf chameleon, *B. pumilum*, or scattered fairly evenly over large areas, as in Jackson's chameleon, *T. jacksonii*. In some individuals, the larger stud-like scales may be coloured differently from the smaller scales that surround them, whereas in others a colour pattern is superimposed over all the scales, regardless of size.

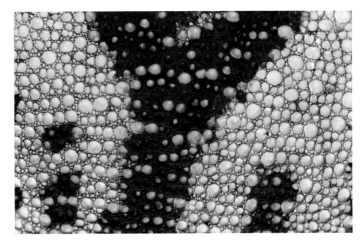

ABOVE A close-up of the different-sized scales of a panther chameleon shows how they are scattered in a seemingly random arrangement.

BELOW The dorsal crest of the Namaqua chameleon, *Chamaeleo namaquensis*, consists of a series of square-shaped knobs.

Specialised scales are found along the dorsal ridge and the mid-ventral line in many species. Dorsal crests can consist of regularly spaced, pointed or conical scales, or the row of specialised scales may be continuous, like the teeth of a saw. In some

RIGHT The rare and unusual spiny-sided chameleon, *Trioceros laterispinis*, from the mountains of eastern Tanzania, is well camouflaged when resting among the lichen-covered branches that form its habitat.

BELOW A small group of West African chameleons, of which the crested chameleon, *Trioceros cristatus* is the best known, have a high dorsal 'fin', which is larger in males than females.

case the crests extend onto the tail. The crest of the Namaqua chameleon, *Chamaeleo namaquensis*, consists of widely spaced squarish or knob-like processes, each made up of several tuberculate scales. The spiny-sided chameleon, *Trioceros laterispinis*, which comes from the Udzungwa Mountains of Tanzania, has a crest consisting of about 16 large, thorn-like scales down its back and a number of less regularly spaced spines on its tail. This species is cryptically coloured greyish-green and bears a striking resemblance to a piece of lichen-covered twig.

Members of the *Brookesia* genus do not have a dorsal crest (nor even a dorsal ridge in many species) but several species in this genus have rows of enlarge scales on either side of their back. In some species, such as *B. brygooi* and *B. perarmata*, these are especially well developed and form a series of spines either side of the dorsal midline. *B. perarmata* has an additional row of conical structures formed from clusters of scales along its flanks.

The West African crested chameleon, *Trioceros cristatus*, has a high fleshy dorsal crest supported by spines that project from its vertebrae. This 'sailfin', which has a scalloped margin, is present in both sexes, but is slightly higher in males, and is reminiscent of the similar structure sported by the dinosaur *Spinosaurus*. A small group of closely related species from West Africa, such as *T. montium*, have similar crests but they are not as well developed. The purpose of the crest is not known.

ABOVE The stomach-striped chameleon, *Calumma gastrotaenia*, has a pair of white lines that run from its chin, along its underside and down its tail.

LEFT Like all reptiles, chameleons need to periodically replace their outer epidermis. When moulting or sloughing their skins chameleons, like most lizards, tend to lose it in several or many pieces, whereas snakes generally shed their skins in one piece.

In some species, a single row of enlarged scales may run along the underside, forming a ventral crest. In the dwarf chameleons, *Bradypodion*, and some *Trioceros* species, these scales can be greatly enlarged on the chameleon's chin, often likened to a beard, and are known as gular crests. The stomach-striped chameleon, *Calumma gastrotaenia*, and some of its close relatives, have, instead of a ventral crest, a pair of thin white lines running the length of their underside.

LEFT The veiled chameleon, *Chamaeleo calyptratus*, has the highest casque of all species, but it is only present in males.

BELOW Several members of the genus *Calumma*, like the Malthe chameleon, *Calumma malthe* have large fleshy flaps or occipital lobes over the neck region and these can be spread as a threat during conflicts or displays.

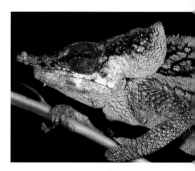

OPPOSITE The top of chameleons' heads are invariably bony and often ornamented with crests and casques whereas that of the female lesser chameleon is decorated with patches of colourful scales.

HEAD ORNAMENTATION

The basic structure of the head in chameleons features a bony ridge that starts on the snout and divides to arch over each eye. In some species, the two ridges merge together again on the top of the head to form a central ridge whereas in other species the central ridge is separate. In either case, the central ridge is often high, forming a bony structure known as a casque. This is better developed in some species than in others and, where present, is invariably larger in males than in females. A common theme is for this casque to be angled back over the nape of the lizard's neck and, in some species, such as the veiled chameleon, *Chamaeleo calyptratus*, and Von Höhnel's chameleon, *Trioceros hoehnelii*, it can be greatly enlarged to form a helmet-like structure. Species belonging to the genus *Calumma* also have a pair of fleshy flaps extending backwards from the head and the chameleon can spread these during displays.

Other species have horns and similar appendages on their heads and snouts. Several *Brookesia* species, including *B. superciliaris* and *B. vadoni*, have pointed

OPPOSITE The 'eyebrow horns' of the leaf chameleon, *Brookesia superciliaris* are particularly exaggerated and almost certainly enhance their ability to blend into their leaf-litter environment.

RIGHT Relative to its size, the lance-nosed chameleon, *Calumma gallus* from eastern Madagascar, probably has the longest 'nose horn' or rostral protuberance of any chameleon species.

BELOW Male lesser chameleons, *Furcifer minor*, have a pair of fleshy horns protruding from their snouts. They are not present in females of this species.

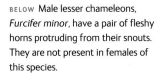

'eyebrows', the purpose of which is thought to break up the outline of the chameleon's eye, which is often used as a 'search' image by predators, when it is at rest. Many species from several genera have horns of some sort. These are of two basic types. They may consist of a single fleshy protuberance, as in the males of the nose-horned chameleon, *Calumma nasutum*, the well-named lance-nosed chameleon, *C. gallus*, and rhinoceros chameleon, *Furcifer rhinoceratus*, all from Madagascar, and *Rhampholeon gorongosae*, from Mozambique, for example. Others, such as *C. furcifer*, *F. minor* and *F. petteri*, all from Madagascar, have a pair of protuberances. Their purpose is thought to be primarily species recognition and, secondarily, to help give the chameleon an outline that is not obviously that of a lizard, and therefore not easy for a predator to spot. They are always larger in males, sometimes lacking altogether in females.

In some of the larger chameleons, however, the head ornamentation is a bony structure consisting of a single horn, or a cluster of horns. These may be quite small and inconspicuous, as in the panther chameleon, *Furcifer pardalis*, or slightly larger and more obvious, as in Parson's chameleon, *Calumma parsonii*, both from Madagascar. In these species the horns are not

RIGHT Male O'Shaughnessy's chameleon, *Calumma oshaughnessyi*, have a short, bony structure on their snout that is absent in females.

RIGHT Male O'Shaughnessy's chameleon, *Calumma oshaughnessyi*, have a short, bony structure on their snout that is absent in females.

made up of a single modified scale but consist of a bony process covered in smaller scales. The horns of several African species, such as those of Fischer's chameleon, *Kinyongia fischeri*, the Uluguru chameleon, *K. uluguruensis*, and the Rwenzori plate-nosed chameleon, *K. xenorhina* (whose specific name means 'strange-nosed'), also fit this description: *Kinyongia* species of this type are sometimes called blade-horned chameleons because their horns are flattened.

Members of the East and West African genus *Trioceros* may or may not have horns, which is rather confusing considering their generic name (which means 'three-horned') but, where present, each horn consists of a single, large, modified scale and is annulated. The number of horns is dependent on species and ranges from none to four or more. Von Höhnel's chameleon, *T. hoehnelii*, for instance, has no horns; Meller's chameleon, *T. melleri*, has a single horn; the Cameroon two-horned mountain chameleon, *T. montium*, has a pair of horns; Jackson's chameleon, *T. jacksonii*, and Johnston's chameleon, *T. johnstoni*, each have three horns; and the imaginatively named four-horned chameleon, *T. quadricornis* has four, as you might expect. Interestingly, though, this latter species may occasionally have six horns, as the horns are arranged as pairs on its snout and some individuals develop a third, smaller pair, just behind the two main pairs. Owen's three-horned chameleon, *T. oweni*, is equally variable; whereas individuals from Cameroon and neighbouring countries have three horns, some of those from further south and east have but a single horn, and are known as the '*unicornis* form'. These structures, regardless of how many there are, appear to be used in combat by males, when they literally 'lock horns' in an attempt to overpower their rivals and dislodge them from their perches. Females of these species have only rudimentary horns, sometimes little more than enlarged scales.

LEFT Male Jackson's chameleons, *Trioceros jacksonii*, have three conspicuous horns that are used in combat and which give the genus its name. Other members of the genus however, have only one, two or even no horns.

LEFT Females Jackson's chameleons, in contrast to the males, have only rudimentary horns, often just three enlarged scales.

EYES

Chameleons' upper and lower eyelids are largely fused together leaving only a small aperture, the position of which can be adjusted, so the whole structure is akin to a rotating gun turret. In addition, the eyes can be rotated independently of each other, so the chameleon can be looking forwards and over its shoulder at the same time. The information gathered by each eye is processed separately; the brain processes the signals sent to it by the left and right eye alternately, at approximately one second intervals – a very clever solution. Only when it is hunting does a chameleon bring both eyes to bear on its prey at the same time, presumably to judge distance, although chameleons can also judge distance using only one eye if necessary, by monitoring the degree of accommodation necessary to focus the lens. Experiments have shown that one-eyed chameleons can hunt almost as efficiently as those in which both eyes are fully functional, although it takes them some time to become proficient.

ABOVE As in all chameleons, the eyelids of Parson's chameleon, *Calumma parsonii* have fused into a single structure and cover the large eye ball, with the aperture size only sufficiently large in diameter to accommodate the pupil and iris.

OPPOSITE The ability to use their independently rotating eyes to look in two directions at the same time, is one of the chameleon's more celebrated abilities. When hunting, they often use one eye to look 'over their shoulder' immediately before focusing both eyes on their prey for the purpose of judging distance.

ABOVE When a chameleon takes aim at an intended victim, the tongue apparatus moves upwards and forwards in the mouth. As the tongue is 'primed', just prior to firing, the chameleon appears to be blowing bubblegum.

RIGHT A chameleon's projectile tongue is one of its most remarkable adaptations. It accelerates from the mouth towards its target at over 450 m per second. When the tongue is deployed, most individuals achieve a hit rate of around 90%.

TONGUE

Chameleons use another unique characteristic – their tongue – when feeding. Their tongues are very long and greatly extensible. A feeding chameleon can shoot its tongue out to a length equal to, or exceeding, its body length. When not in use, the tongue rests on the floor of the chameleon's mouth and extends back into its throat. As it prepares to launch its tongue the chameleon first

moves it upwards and forwards so that its tip is at the front of its mouth, and protruding slightly. It aims by turning its whole head and pointing its snout at the prey. Finally, muscles around the tongue contract causing it to expand and shoot out rapidly. The prey is captured by the rounded tip and immediately withdrawn back into the chameleon's mouth at great speed. The tip is not sticky but secures the prey by suction. The chameleon uses its powerful jaws to crush the prey before swallowing.

COLOUR

Chameleons' most famous characteristic is their ability to change colour, but this is often misunderstood. Claims that chameleons can take on a tartan pattern if placed on a piece of plaid, for instance, have no basis in fact, and their ability to mimic their background is limited to lighter or darker coloration. Indeed, coloration is affected far more by temperature and mood than by the background. When cold, chameleons turn dark and will angle their bodies to a heat source – usually the sun – in order to absorb radiant warmth more quickly. Once they have reached their preferred temperature they turn a lighter shade, often green, yellowish-green or bluish-green, depending largely on species, but to some extent also on sex, age and geographic location. Chameleons also change colour during social interactions and these changes can be very dramatic. Two males confronting one another will suddenly become brighter, while colour patterns that were previously hidden or insignificant may emerge as vivid stripes, blotches and spots. Females also change colour when they see a male: sometimes as a submissive gesture or, alternatively, to show that they have already mated and contain developing eggs. These patterns often bear no resemblance to their normal coloration. Females of the jewelled chameleon, *Furcifer lateralis*, Labord's chameleon, *F. labordi*, and a few closely related species, as well as female veiled chameleons, *Chamaeleo calyptratus*, for instance, turn almost black save for scattered spots of bright blue, yellow and red. A change of this kind, known as gravid coloration, is a well-known phenomenon in related agamids and iguanids, although it has not been as widely investigated in chameleons.

BELOW Famed for their ability to change colour, many chameleons routinely display a riotous kaleidoscope of colour like this montane jewel chameleon, *Furcifer campani* from the highlands of Madagascar.

The key to all these colour changes, regardless of their causes, is the presence of specialised cells in the epidermis known as chromatophores and melanophores. They are arranged as layers. The uppermost layer contains two types: erythrophores – cells with red pigment – and xanthophores – cells with yellow pigment. The next layer down contains iridiophores, which contain the white or colourless pigment, guanine (and so they are sometimes known as guanophores). The iridiophores reflect light, especially in the blue part of the spectrum. If the light reflected from the iridiophores passes through yellow pigment-containing cells in the upper layer the colour appears as green (blue filtered through yellow), otherwise it remains blue. Both colours are well represented in chameleons. Below the iridiophore-containing layer is an even deeper one, populated by melanophores, which are cells containing granules of the black pigment melanin. These granules can clump together or spread out within the cells, causing groups of scales to become lighter or darker quite rapidly. When they spread out, the dark colour they produce obscures the brighter colours produced by the two upper layers. These cells are controlled by the nervous system and react in response to a variety of stimuli.

The small species, members of the subfamily Brookesiinae, that live in the forests of Madagascar (*Brookesia*) and Central and East Africa (*Rhampholeon* and *Rieppeleon*) are not colourful and neither do they have the capacity to change colour, other than becoming slightly darker when they are cold. They are predominantly brown and it is no coincidence that these species look like dead leaves. Here, the melanophores are the most important source of colour and the other types of colour-producing cells are few in number or absent altogether.

ABOVE The intense coloration and vivid pattern of this excited male lesser chameleon, *Furcifer minor*, coupled with the distended throat and flattened body, are all intended to make it look larger and more impressive to females, rival males or potential predators. It can switch this pattern on and off in a matter of seconds.

LEGS AND FEET

Chameleons' legs are proportionately long and project downwards, rather than splaying out to the side, as is more common in lizards. This allows them to walk in an upright posture, with their feet tucked under the body and each foot arranged in a line, as is essential when they are walking along a thin branch, for instance. Coupled to this method of walking and climbing is the arrangement of their toes, which is unique to chameleons. Although they have a total of five on each foot, these are fused into groups of three and two. On the front feet the bundle of three is on the inside, whereas on the hind feet the bundle of three is on the outside. The two bundles on each foot are opposed to each other so that the feet are shaped like pincers, allowing them to grasp thin twigs and branches. Chameleons typically walk with a slow, deliberate gait, in keeping with their strategy of trying to escape notice, and may rock backwards and forwards as they move, to simulate the effect of a leaf being moved by the breeze. If necessary, chameleons can run more quickly for short distances, and the mainly terrestrial Namaqua chameleon, *Chamaeleo namaquensis*, is among the more athletic species.

Each of the five toes ends in a small claw, which helps in climbing, especially when the surface is too broad to be clasped by the feet. The soles of chameleons' feet are covered in small, rough scales except in members of the genera *Brookesia* and *Rieppeleon*, in which the scales are pointed, giving them a prickly surface. In both cases, the shape of these specialised scales is thought to improve their grip. In some species of *Chamaeleo*, males have a spur projecting from the back of their hind feet, which looks like a vestigial toe but which is thought to play a role during mating.

OPPOSITE Chameleons' toes are fused into two bundles, which are arranged opposite one another, allowing them to grip thin branches with ease.

ABOVE Even the minute feet of a leaf chameleon, *Brookesia* sp. have the capability to grip and allow these chameleons to climb, to a limited extent.

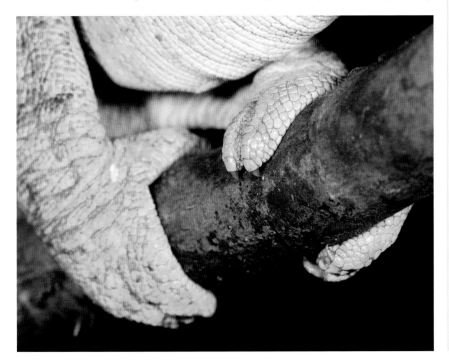

LEFT The hind feet of this Parson's chameleon, *Calumma parsonii* clearly show the fused toes, with a group of three on the outside.

THE TAIL

The larger, more arboreal species have long, prehensile tails, which are as long as their head and body combined. They use these to help balance and to grasp twigs and branches, as a fifth limb. A climbing chameleon is able to support the weight of its body with its tail once it is firmly anchored, and will often reach down with its body and limbs while gripping a higher branch with its tail. The scales on the undersurface of the tail often end in short bristles and conical structures, giving them a better grip (the tails of some arboreal geckos are similarly equipped). Resting and sleeping chameleons usually carry their tails coiled, like a clock spring. Small species, members of the Brookesiinae, have relatively short tails, and are sometimes called 'stump-tailed' chameleons, although Marshall's pygmy chameleon, *Rhampholeon marshalli*, from Zimbabwe and Mozambique, has quite a long tail. These chameleons' tails are probably not prehensile in the true sense of the term but they do use their tails to steady themselves while climbing.

CHAPTER 3

Enemies and defence

BECAUSE CHAMELEONS ARE SOLITARY and generally difficult to detect, it might seem logical to assume they rarely feature prominently on the menus of other animals. While this holds true in some instances, there are a good number of predators that either target chameleons at various times or take them opportunistically.

Avoiding detection is a chameleon's principle means of self-preservation and should this fail there are any number of predators quick to take advantage. In general, these include typical small carnivores like mongooses, civets and genets, a wide range of birds, and some other reptiles, especially certain species of snake. What is more, it is not just adult chameleons that are susceptible: both their eggs and newly emerged young are particularly vulnerable at times.

OPPOSITE The boomslang, *Dispholidus typus,* is almost exclusively arboreal. It has binocular vision and can spot potential prey before it moves. The snake efficiently dispatches its prey with potent venom. Arboreal lizards, especially chameleons, are prominent in its diet.

BELOW The Madagascar cat snake, *Madagascariophis colubrinus,* is a common nocturnal species that kills by constriction. Here it is swallowing a small warty chameleon, *Furcifer verrucosus.*

TYPES OF PREDATORS

While no predators could realistically be described as chameleon specialists, there are a number of arboreal snake and bird species that target lizards in general and chameleons may feature significantly. In eastern and southern Africa, the boomslang, *Dispholidus typus,* and vine or twig snakes, genus *Thelotornis,* are specialist arboreal hunters that certainly prey upon chameleons regularly, the latter species possessing binocular vision that greatly aids the detection of motionless chameleons.

In Madagascar there are several colubrid snakes that fill broadly similar arboreal niches to the African species mentioned, and these also include chameleons in their diet. The bizarre leaf-nosed or spear-nosed snakes, genus *Langaha,* frequent low-level bushes and trees and are skilful lizard hunters that are known to eat *Brookesia* and small *Calumma* species, like *C. nasutum.* Similarly, the nocturnal Malagasy 'cat' snakes, genera *Stenophis* and *Madagascariophis,* are frequent predators of small to medium-sized chameleon species.

The harmless 'fandrefiala', *Ithycyphus perineti*, is a moderate to large arboreal snake that is feared by many rural Malagasy people, who believe the snake has the power to mesmerise any person or cattle passing beneath it. The snake can then stiffen its body into a spear, before dropping from above to impale the victim. This rather fanciful belief is an obvious consequence of the snake's appearance: it is pale yellow-brown, with a blood-red rear third and tail. What is not myth is the snake's ability to catch larger species of chameleon. In rainforest areas the short-horned chameleon, *Calumma brevicorne*, and Parson's chameleon, *C. parsonii*, are known victims, while in drier areas species like Oustalet's chameleon, *Furcifer oustaleti*, and warty chameleon, *F. verrucosus*, are taken. This snake's congener, *I. oursi*, from the drier regions of southwest Madagascar is also a chameleon hunter.

In Africa a number of bird groups are significant lizard predators and consequently take chameleons. At the larger end of the spectrum these include the ground hornbills, genus *Bucorvus*, and smaller bush and woodland hornbill species belonging to the genus *Tockus*, such as African grey hornbill, *T. nasutus*, and Von der Decken's hornbill, *T. deckeni*.

A number of small to medium–large raptors are also notable predators; these include reptile specialists like the various species of snake eagle (genus *Circaetus*) and lizard buzzard, *Kaupifalco monogrammicus*, together with more generalist hunters like the augur buzzard, *Buteo augur*, chanting-goshawks, genus *Melierax*, and various smaller goshawks and sparrowhawks, genus *Accipiter*.

Among smaller birds the predatory behaviour of true shrikes, genus *Lanius*, is renowned, particularly their habit of impaling victims. While in most species insects

form the bulk of their diet, some of the more robust shrikes do tackle vertebrate prey and are known to 'punch well above their weight' when overcoming victims as much as three to five times heavier than themselves. Relatively large prey encompasses small mammals, snakes and various lizards, including chameleons. Several different shrikes occur in the grasslands and woodlands of East Africa and a number of these like common fiscal, *L. collaris*, long-tailed fiscal, *L. cababisi*, and woodchat shrike, *L. senator*, have been observed with smaller chameleons, sometimes impaled on thorns.

Also renowned is the thick-set, grey-headed bush-shrike, *Malaconotus blanchoti*, which inhabits woodland and bushland in many of the drier regions of sub-Saharan Africa. Endowed with a powerful, strongly hooked bill, it can tackle larger species such as flap-necked chameleon, *Chamaeleo dilepis*, which it beats to death against a branch, before wedging the victim between twigs and tearing it apart.

In Madagascar, some of the larger endemic vangas, family Vangidae, have evolved similar habits. This is especially true in species like helmet vanga, *Euryceros prevostii*, which lives only in the pristine rainforests of the northeast, and the hook-billed vanga, *Vanga curvirostris*, and rufous vanga, *Schetba rufa*, which occur in both eastern rainforests and western dry forests. As a family, the vangas are famous for the variety of their beak sizes and shapes. The larger, more predatory species are equipped with heavy, strong beaks with hooked tips that allow them to tackle a variety of vertebrates including chameleons and other lizards. Their hunting methods are similar: perching in the understorey for long periods, while scouring the vicinity for potential food. Once located, prey is snatched or seized from its substrate before the bird returns to its perch to eat the meal. Hook-billed vangas often wedge chameleons in a tree fork, before pulling off the victim's limbs, whereas helmet and rufous vangas secure chameleons and other similarly large prey with one or both feet and then use their bill to tear off manageable pieces. These vangas are all opportunists and will prey upon both arboreal chameleon species, genera *Calumma* and *Furcifer*, and the much smaller, cryptic, forest-floor-dwelling leaf chameleons, genus *Brookesia*.

LEFT The helmet vanga, *Euryceros prevostii*, is Madagascar's equivalent of a small hornbill and often takes small chameleons.

RIGHT The scaly ground roller, *Brachypteracias squamiger*, is one of four ground rollers endemic to Madagascar's rainforests that preys on a variety of small reptiles, including chameleons, especially *Brookesia* sp.

Other endemic Malagasy groups whose diets include smaller chameleons are the ground-rollers, family Brachypteraciidae, which feed primarily by picking through leaf-litter and low foliage (hence leaf chameleons, genus *Brookesia*, feature strongly in their diet) and the couas, subfamily Couinae, some members of which are terrestrial forest-floor-feeders, while others are mainly arboreal hunters.

As on mainland Africa, there are a number of small and medium-sized raptors that eat chameleons occasionally, for instance Madagascar sparrowhawk, *Accipiter madagascariensis*, Madagascar cuckoo-falcon, *Aviceda madagascariensis*, and Madagascar buzzard, *Buteo brachypterus*. However, two larger raptors warrant specific mention.

Studies of the endangered Madagascar serpent eagle, *Eutriorchis astur*, in the rainforests of the Masoala peninsula, found that a high proportion of prey items brought back to the nest for developing chicks were larger species of forest chameleon. Similarly, over 65% of prey items being brought to a nest of a pair of Madagascar harrier-hawks, *Polybroides radiatus*, also on the Masoala peninsula, were large species like panther chameleon, *Furcifer pardalis*, and Parson's chameleon, *Calumma parsonii*. Madagascar harrier-hawks are broadly distributed around all native forest areas on the island and it is doubtful that chameleons feature so significantly at other localities.

There are a number of endemic carnivores on Madagascar from the family Eupleridae that take chameleons from time to time. These include smaller species like the narrow-striped mongoose, *Mungotictis decemlineata*, and ring-tailed mongoose, *Galidia elegans*, and the island's largest carnivore, the fosa, *Cryptoprocta ferox*. Interestingly, there is also a record of a ring-tailed lemur, *Lemur catta*, catching and eating a jewelled chameleon, *Furcifer lateralis*, although it is doubtful such morsels constitute a regular part of this primate's diet, including adults of the same species.

LEFT Madagascar's ring-tailed mongoose, *Galidia elegans*, is an opportunistic chameleon hunter.

BELOW While larger prey like lemurs constitute the majority of the diet of the fosa, *Cryptoprocta ferox*, madagascar's largest carnivore will also take a variety of smaller prey including chameleons.

Of course, chameleons may also be eaten at other stages in their life-cycle. They routinely lay clutches of 30 or more eggs, which offer rich pickings for any predator capable of discovering such a bounty. In Africa large terrestrial lizards like monitors, genus *Varanus*, are adept at finding and excavating chameleon nests. Several mammalian carnivores do likewise opportunistically; these include the African civet, *Civettictis civetta*, honey badger or ratel, *Mellivora capensis*, and bush pig, *Potamochoerus larvatus*. In Madagascar, along with bush pigs, the hog-nosed snakes, genus *Leioheterodon*, are skilful egg raiders, targeting not only the buried nests of chameleons but also of Malagasy iguanid lizards, genus *Oplurus*.

From the moment they hatch, as perfect miniature versions of their parents, baby chameleons have to fend for themselves. Even the newborn of the largest species (Parson's chameleon, *Calumma parsonii*, and Oustalet's chameleon, *Furcifer oustaleti*) are barely larger than a fingernail and the young of smaller species are miniscule. All baby chameleons are confronted by dangers from predators inhabiting this Lilliputian world. These predators include a variety of larger spiders and mantises that are easily capable of overpowering a hatchling chameleon, a host of

different snakes and birds that are small prey specialists, larger frogs, rats and shrews and even colonies of predatory ants. Being small also means that young chameleons are potential prey to larger chameleons, including adults of the same species.

As well as the various larger predators that attack chameleons, they are also subject to disease and parasitism from smaller organisms. As a general rule, the most effective parasites are those that have little effect on their host and chameleons' parasite burdens are rarely heavy under natural conditions. Chameleons that are captured and transported within the pet trade however, often contain large infestations of parasites due to their stressed condition, and most of what is known about chameleon parasites comes from screening of captive individuals.

A variety of internal and external parasites have been found. Ticks and mites occur only rarely on chameleons, even though they may be common on closely related lizards; indeed, related lizards have special 'mite pockets'. These are areas of skin that lack scales, attracting mites into one small area for reasons that are unclear at present, although various theories have been put forward. Nevertheless, they have not evolved in chameleons, possibly because they shed their skin more frequently than other species.

BELOW This rhinoceros chameleon, *Furcifer rhinoceratus*, is infested with a long roundworm, which can clearly be seen under its skin in front of its hind leg. Parasites of this type are common in wild populations but probably do little harm.

Internal parasites include protozoans, such as amoebas, flagellates, and coccidian species, all of which reside in the intestines and are transmitted through ingestion of eggs. (As an aside, parasites of this type are rare in wild populations but often thrive under crowded and unhygienic captive conditions because their eggs have a far greater chance of being re-ingested than they would otherwise.) Other protozoans are transmitted through blood-sucking insects, notably mosquitoes, and also other biting insects. These include well-known blood parasites such as *Plasmodium* (causing malaria) and *Trypanosoma* species (causing sleeping sickness in humans) and both of these have been found in chameleons, although they are not thought to significantly affect their health.

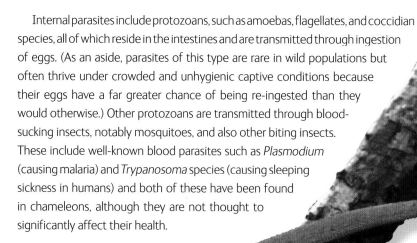

Larger internal parasites consist mainly of forms of nematodes, including roundworms, lungworms and filarid worms, all of which are commonly present in wild chameleons. The main source of infestation with these worms is probably ingestion via a food species, and, while some of them remain in the intestines, others migrate out of the gut and into the bloodstream before moving into other organs. Filarid worms, for instance, often move into the subcutaneous region of the chameleon where they are visible as long, coiled structures just under the chameleon's skin.

While all species of chameleon are undoubtedly preyed on, the overall effect of predation and impact on populations is limited. Their capacity to produce large numbers of young, their largely solitary existence and their ability to conceal themselves so effectively means predation overall has a moderate effect. That said,

ABOVE In the Kenyan highlands the populations of Von Höhnel's chameleon, *Trioceros hoehnelii*, regularly experience boom and bust cycles. The reasons behind these dramatic population fluctuations are unclear, but may be linked to predation cycles.

there is some evidence of 'boom and bust' population dynamics with some species. In East Africa, there are areas where shrikes and other conspicuous and numerous birds like starlings seem to develop a taste for certain chameleons, in particular the small to medium-sized bush-dwelling species, and the chameleons' populations apparently experience regular peak and crash cycles. For example, sometimes in the Kenyan highlands, Von Höhnel's chameleon, *Trioceros hoehnelii*, can be encountered in large numbers, with five or six individuals prominent on most if not all bushes in an area, but at other times the same bushes are devoid of them. Such cyclical changes, where populations explode and crash, has also been noted in the dwarf chameleons, genus *Bradypodion*, from southern Africa. It is thought that such apparently dramatic fluctuations may be linked in some way with predation.

DEFENCE STRATEGIES

A chameleon's best defence against predation is to avoid being detected. For a long time it was thought that their spectacular ability to change colour was primarily associated with camouflage. It is certainly without doubt that many chameleons are able to match the colours and hues of their immediate environment very closely, and these changes are influenced by fluctuations in light, shade and temperature. However, we now know this is a secondary function and that colour change is primarily related to communication, whether expressions of dominance and submission, mood and emotion or courtship. Body shape and movement are also keys to maintaining their deception.

ABOVE Unlike all other species, the largely terrestrial Namaqua chameleon, *Chamaeleo namaquensis*, is fast enough over ground to be able to flee danger.

OPPOSITE Male panther chameleons, *Furcifer pardalis*, have particularly impressive threat displays when trying to scare off would be attackers or intruders.

So, if concealment fails and chameleons are confronted by a threat, do they have any further tricks up their sleeve? Well some, but not many. Chameleons cannot run from danger (with one exception, the Namaqua chameleon, *Chamaeleo namaquensis*, see below) so their only active physical defences are hissing and biting. The remaining alternatives are behavioural and include surreptitiously moving around to maintain the branch they are on between themselves and danger, feigning death, and in extreme circumstances leaping from their branch.

The Namaqua chameleon is the only species that is truly terrestrial. It lives in the semi-arid and desert regions along the southwest coast of southern Africa, including the Namib Desert and Skeleton Coast. This is one of the driest regions on Earth and offers little in the way of cover. Hence, unlike every other species, the Namaqua chameleon is able to run, at considerable speed, from danger.

When approached, larger species like the flap-necked chameleon, *Chamaeleo dilepis*, Oustalet's chameleon, *Furcifer oustaleti*, and panther chameleon, *F. pardalis*, may adopt impressive threat displays, where they inflate and laterally compress their bodies to look as large as possible, hiss loudly, distend their throat pouches, gape

BELOW Brygoo's leaf chameleon, *Brookesia brygooi*, like all Malagasy leaf chameleons, is amazingly well camouflaged amongst the leaf litter.

BOTTOM By inflating its lungs, laterally compressing its body and erecting its gular (throat) pouch, the threat display of this *Furcifer antimena* is designed to intimidate.

widely to expose a brightly coloured oral interior and raise their occipital flaps to further intimidate. If this fails, they are able to administer a powerful, but ultimately harmless, bite.

Several species of East African leaf chameleon, genera *Rhampholeon* and *Rieppeleon*, have evolved a distinctive and unusual defence mechanism: when held they apparently vibrate, in a way that can feel like a mild electric shock. This is probably the consequence of the chameleon exhaling air in minute amounts and is presumably designed to startle any would-be predator into releasing its intended

victim. This behaviour has also been noted, to a lesser extent, in some of the stump-tailed or leaf chameleons in Madagascar, genus *Brookesia*, for instance *B. ebenaui*.

Other species are known to 'feign death', lying on their backs completely still (known as thanatosis) in the hope that a predator will loose interest. Several species of *Brookesia* adopt this technique, including *B. superciliaris* and *B. decaryi*. A variation on this theme is the so-called 'freeze and roll' response, where forest-floor species when approached or sensing vibrations from something potentially hazardous, curl up immobile, then roll away down the slope they happen to be on.

This ploy is adopted by the smallest of all chameleons, *B. minima, B. peyrierasi* and *B. exarmata* among others.

Many larger species choose to sleep at the very extremities of branches, in an attempt to reduce the likelihood of predation, especially from arboreal snakes. Should a predator attempt to creep up on the sleeping chameleon it would have to do so extremely surreptitiously in order to succeed, as the chameleon's automatic response to feeling any vibrations is to instantly relax its grip with all four feet and drop to the ground to make good its escape.

CHAPTER 4
Food and feeding

CHAMELEONS ARE ALMOST EXCLUSIVELY CARNIVOROUS, and are able to catch a wide variety of prey. In most species the diet is dominated by invertebrates, especially insects, but larger chameleons are able to tackle smaller vertebrates. Three species do occasionally eat leaves and fruit. Chameleons rarely, if ever, drink from still water; instead they prefer to lap at rainwater droplets or dewdrops that form on foliage.

TYPES OF PREY

Given that chameleons range in size from the diminutive pygmy leaf chameleons *Brookesia micra* and *B. minima*, which have total lengths of less than 35 mm (1 ⅓ in), to the substantial and impressive Parson's chameleon, *Calumma parsonii*, and Oustalet's

OPPOSITE All chameleons are voracious hunters. Large species like this panther chameleon, *Furcifer pardalis* can eat upwards of 20–30 substantial insects or invertebrates in a day. This one has caught a large praying mantis.

LEFT Chameleons rarely drink from standing water, preferring instead to lap at dew or rainwater droplets that collect on leaves and other vegetation.

and Oustalet's chameleon, *Furcifer oustaleti*, which both attain lengths greater than 60 cm (24 in), it is not surprising that the prey targeted varies dramatically in size too.

The smaller species, especially the leaf chameleons, genera *Rhampholeon*, *Rieppeleon* and *Brookesia*, principally inhabit forest-floor environments and spend the majority of the day hunting among leaf-litter. Hence, their diets are dominated by tiny prey such as mites, termites, springtails, small ants and first or second instar larvae of larger insects.

The vast majority of chameleons are arboreal, with the bulk of their diets dominated by various insects and other arthropods, especially grasshoppers, locusts, other orthopterans, beetles, butterflies, moths, stick insects and mantises.

The very largest chameleons are even capable of subduing vertebrate prey. While such items only constitute a minor part of their diet, lizards, including small or juvenile chameleons, small birds and small mammals obviously provide a significant amount of nutrition.

While the diet of two desert-dwelling species, the veiled chameleon, *Chamaeleo calyptratus*, and Namaqua chameleon, *C. namaquensis*, consists primarily of insects they will occasionally consume the leaves, flowers and fruit of various plants. This is especially true in times of drought, when water is scarce. Jackson's chameleon, *Trioceros jacksonii*, which is restricted to some highland forest areas in Kenya and Tanzania, has also been recorded eating plant matter.

FEEDING TECHNIQUES

The chameleon's hunting technique is unique and has led to the evolution of perhaps its two most famous and distinctive attributes, independently swivelling eyes and a projectile tongue.

Virtually all chameleons are stealth hunters, the only exception being the Namaqua chameleon, *Chamaeleo namaquensis*, which actively pursues prey on some occasions. However, the vast majority, either move very deliberately along branches and through foliage, or rest motionless, systematically searching their surroundings, with each eye roving over all areas both in front and behind. Once a meal has been spotted, the chameleon turns its head towards the prey and rotates each eye to face forwards looking at the intended victim. With both eyes focused, the chameleon attains stereoscopic vision and can judge distance and perceive depth accurately. Chameleons also often rock back and forth, which presumably helps fine-tune the range data to the prey. This is crucial to success, as the information is assimilated and used to guide the tongue accurately towards the prey.

With both eyes fully operational, a chameleon achieves around a 90% hit rate. The 'tongue firing and chew' response appears to be 'hard-wired' as a chameleon will automatically begin chewing once the tongue recoils back into the mouth, even if it fails to catch the prey. Chameleons that are blind in one eye can still hunt but their success rate is severely reduced, although they learn to cope better with time.

OPPOSITE When actively hunting, chameleons search their surroundings with constantly roving eyes, with each eye scanning a field of view that covers 180° from front to back, giving complete all round vision. With each eye looking in different directions they have to assimilate two separate images. Only when a potential victim has been pinpointed, do the eyes focus together.

ABOVE While chameleons are heavily reliant on their stereoscopic vision when hunting, individuals that become blind in one eye can with time learn to adapt and remain successful hunters.

In a series of controlled experiments a number of chameleons were temporarily rendered blind in one eye (using a small patch) and then given the opportunity to hunt. On the first day, the one-eyed chameleons registered zero success, on day two they managed to hit 20% of their targets and by the fourth day this had risen to above 50%. Chameleons permanently blind in one eye usually attain a 65% strike rate over time.

The sequence of prey capture can be broken down into four phases. Firstly, the prey range is assessed and the primed tongue begins to emerge slowly from the mouth (the chameleon looks like it is blowing bubblegum). Second, the tongue accelerates forwards at lightning speed (up to 490 m or 1,600 ft per second). Third, the tongue pad decelerates to hit and grasp the target, and, finally, the tongue withdraws back into the mouth clutching the prey.

The tongue mechanism has fascinated and perplexed scientists ever since these lizards were first discovered. The basic statistics are quite remarkable. The tongue can extend to up to one and a half times the length of the chameleon's body, hit and adhere to a small, sometimes moving target, and then retract back into the mouth gripping the prize, and all in the blink of an eye.

Early hypotheses suggested the mechanism was pneumatically operated with a hollow tongue rapidly filling with air from the lungs or hydraulically controlled by a speedy inflow of blood. It was not until 1836 that a muscular explanation was first proposed and all subsequent investigations have corroborated this, although it has taken the best part of another one and a half centuries to satisfactorily unravel all the complexities.

The entire apparatus consists of the hollow tongue that sheaths over a cartilaginous spike, known as the entoglossal process, and this all sits at the bottom rear of the mouth. When primed, the tongue slides forwards and upwards to the front of the mouth, like a missile launcher being wheeled into position. The tongue itself has three components: accelerator muscles, retractor muscles and the muscular tongue pad. The accelerator muscles are arranged in concentric rings, with associated collagen fibres that store elastic energy, a bit like a spring-loaded compressed telescope. When a chameleon strikes the elastic energy is released in just 20 milliseconds and the concentric muscles pushing against the entoglossal process force the tongue to extend rapidly.

BELOW Having carefully moved into position, a male panther chameleon, *Furcifer pardalis*, launches its tongue towards an unsuspecting praying mantis.

After it has been deployed, the tongue's range can be controlled to an extent, by tendons that slow it prior to impact and help cushion the blow. The tongue pad is covered with viscous saliva and has a trailing flap of skin. When the pad hits its target, the prey is gripped by a combination of sticky saliva and muscle, and then by the flap of skin that continues its forward motion to envelop the victim.

At this point the retractor muscles come into play. They sit to the rear of the accelerator muscles, also around the cartilaginous entoglossal process, like a concertina, and passively extend when the tongue is fired. After impact, they contract and draw in the tongue and prey, like bellows compressing. Prey is then chewed before being swallowed.

BELOW Chameleons' jaws are powerful enough to overpower and masticate insects with hard exoskeletons such as grasshoppers and beetles.

As an interesting aside, typical lizards in cool environments have to warm themselves considerably to be able to move and hunt effectively. But chameleons, being slow-moving, stealth hunters, are not constrained in the same way by lower temperatures and so can be active early in the day and at lower body temperatures than other lizards in the same habitat. But, do lower temperatures affect their hunting efficiency? It might seem logical to assume that cool conditions would be detrimental to the function of the high-speed tongue. However, recent research has shown that the tongue works efficiently over a wide range of temperatures and a chameleon's hit rates are reduced by only 10% when temperatures fall as low as 15°C (59°F). This would appear to be because the tongue's firing mechanisms rely on an elastic energy system and this performs significantly better at lower temperatures than normal muscles. Hence chameleons have an advantage over other lizards in cool conditions. This may be one explanation as to why chameleons appear to do so well, and reach their greatest levels of diversity, in cooler montane forest environments.

While the chameleon's tongue is obviously an amazing product of evolution that lies at the core of the group's success, it is not without its perils. In suburban gardens in East Africa, there are several records of Von Höhnel's chameleons, *Trioceros hoehnelii*, catching their tongues on rose thorns while feeding, ultimately with fatal consequences!

In general chameleons have a remarkable capacity for feeding, although this is influenced by a number of factors including temperature, emotional/hormonal state and the size of prey being consumed. In the wild, an adult panther chameleon, *Furcifer pardalis*, can consume upwards of 20 grasshoppers in a day.

The Namaqua chameleon, *Chamaeleo namaquensis*, is atypical in many ways, all a consequence of, and adaptation to, the desert environment in which it lives. In deserts, meals do not come along very often, so the Namaqua chameleon cannot afford to be choosy and actively hunts a far broader range of prey than other chameleons. Naturally, desert insects such as Namib beetles, genus *Stenocara*, form a large part of its diet, but other potentially hazardous invertebrates may also become tasty morsels and the chameleon has developed ways to neutralise any threat. For instance, the projectile tongue can be used to strategically target the lower abdomen of wasps or the tail below the sting of scorpions. Once the prey is in its mouth the chameleon chews off the dangerous bits then spits out the entire contents. After examining the corpse to make sure the venomous parts have been separated, the chameleon re-ingests the edible remainder. This chewing and spitting out routine may be repeated several times before the chameleon is convinced the hazard has been removed. Where large scorpions are concerned they are even able to remove the pincers as well.

BELOW With its eyes directed forwards, a Namaqua chameleon begins the process of propelling its tongue rapidly towards its prey.

CHAPTER 5

Reproduction and development

FOR THE MOST PART CHAMELEONS ARE non-social creatures, and they are often downright anti-social, intolerant and aggressive towards one another. There have been some accounts of apparent 'social' behaviour, but this is more akin to the formation of temporary aggregations in a small number of species, rather than strictly social behaviour with established communities and long-term bonds between individuals. For the majority of chameleons, the only time they come into contact with adults of the same species, of either sex, is during courtship and mating.

Species inhabiting environments and habitats without pronounced seasonal variation may breed at any time of the year, whereas in more seasonal regions the period of reproduction generally corresponds to the humid or rainy season. It may be that changing aspects of weather or day length prompt hormonal changes that trigger sexual behaviour. Some species are known to breed more than once annually. For instance, the jewelled chameleon, *Furcifer lateralis*, a common species inhabiting central and western Madagascar, produces two or three clutches, as does the desert-dwelling Namaqua chameleon, *Chamaeleo namaquensis*, while *C. gracilis*, from sub-Saharan Africa, breeds twice annually, once at the end of the wet season and then again in the middle of the dry season.

COURTSHIP

Courtship varies between species, but some generalisations can be made. In many of the larger species, females may advertise their receptiveness, for instance with changes in coloration, or males may simply pursue a potential mate until she acquiesces. Outside the breeding season females often behave very aggressively towards males and quickly turn intense contrasting colours if approached. If this fails to stop the male's advances, she gapes widely and hisses until he retreats. When a female is receptive, all such behaviour

OPPOSITE These two chameleons have worked themselves into a very precarious position while mating. As with most chameleons, the larger male can be very forceful, often grappling with the female and gripping her tightly during copulation.

BELOW A mating pair of Boettger's chameleons, *Calumma boettgeri*, are suspended from a thin branch by the male's tail.

stops and aggression is replaced with a calmer disposition and her pattern and colour becomes more uniform. Once gravid, females, may then adopt another livery, to advertise their condition and prevent unwanted advances from males.

Males may also change colour, in some instances becoming extremely vivid. This may simply be a consequence of transition into reproductive fettle, but may also be in response to other males competing for the attentions of a receptive female. Kaleidoscopic colour change is particularly spectacular in species like the panther chameleon, *Furcifer pardalis*, and veiled chameleon, *Chamaeleo calyptratus*.

Competing males often size one another up, with elaborate posturing, but also readily fight. Species with horn-like nasal appendages or rostral protuberances joust and bite, others simply grapple, bite and hiss while attempting to dislodge their opponent. Conflicts are highly aggressive. As soon as a loser concedes he flees quickly or drops to the ground to escape, preventing the victor pressing home his advantage and causing lasting harm. While basking in glory the victor's colours become increasingly vivid, while the vanquished generally goes dark.

Males of larger species with occipital lobes, like the Malthe chameleon, *Calumma malthe*, and blue-legged chameleon, *C. crypticum*, often splay these during courtship, together with extending their gular sacs, presumably to make themselves more alluring to potential mates.

The courtship ritual of South African dwarf chameleons, genus *Bradypodion*, involves the male's coloration becoming more extravagant, then him approaching a female with pronounced head nodding and rocking movements. Non-receptive females repel such advances with jerky body movements and aggression, while receptive females allow the male to align himself with her and they walk adjacent to one another. After some time, the male mounts the female and is carried on her back until the pair concludes copulation, usually after dark. Similar courtship rituals have also been observed in some of the Malagasy leaf chameleons, genus *Brookesia*, for instance the minute leaf chameleon *B. minima*.

Male head nodding and jerking is also known from some larger Malagasy species like short-horned chameleon, *Calumma brevicorne*, nose-horned chameleon, *C. nasutum*, Parson's chameleon, *C. parsonii* and Wills' chameleon, *Furcifer willsii*.

Mating itself can be a rough affair, with the larger male gripping the female tightly and sometimes biting her back. He mounts her from behind, twisting his tail around and beneath hers, to allow his extruded hemipenis to enter her cloaca. Copulation lasts between 10 and 30 minutes, depending on species. Only one of the male's two hemipenes is used during a single copulation.

ABOVE In many chameleons, the coloration of the female changes dramatically once they have mated successfully and their eggs are developing. This avoids further advances by males. Compare the coloration of this female lesser chameleon, *Furcifer minor*, with that of the same species opposite.

OPPOSITE A female lesser chameleon, *Furcifer minor*, in the normal, receptive coloration. Once gravid, this individual will become much darker, with vividly contrasting patches of bright coloration as seen in the image above.

REPRODUCTION

The majority of chameleons, including all species in Madagascar, are oviparous, that is they lay eggs. A small number of species are ovoviviparous, whereby they bear live young. This is not true live birth as in the case of placental mammals (viviparous), but rather where the female retains the embryos, with each developing in its own membrane sac (effectively an egg without the hard shell). At 'birth' the female deposits

these sacs on vegetation and the young break free and 'hatch' immediately. All dwarf chameleons, genus *Bradypodion*, are ovoviviparous and produce 5 to 15 young, as are some of the larger East African species belonging to the *Trioceros* group. There are around 14 such species, and all are higher altitude montane forest dwellers, like Jackson's chameleon, *T. jacksonii*, although the reasons for this are unclear.

Oviparous species lay clutches that range from 2 to 3 eggs, up to 60 or more. In general smaller species produce smaller clutches, with the larger chameleons being proportionally more productive. For instance, Malagasy leaf chameleons, genus *Brookesia*, lay 2 to 4 eggs; medium-sized species like short-horned chameleon, *Calumma brevicorne*, and panther chameleon, *Furcifer pardalis*, produce clutches of 20 to 25 eggs, while Leviathans such as Parson's chameleon, *C. parsonii*, produce anywhere between 30 and 60 or more eggs.

A chameleon's egg is enclosed in a fibrous envelope (soft shell), which is susceptible to desiccation. Females of most species descend to the ground to dig a nest in damp sand or soil. The depth of the nest varies with species: the panther chameleon, *Furcifer pardalis*, and short-horned chameleon, *Calumma brevicorne*, both excavate nests 10 to 15 cm (4 to 6 in) deep. A handful of *Brookesia* species, for example *B. stumpffi*, lay

ABOVE Unless they are live-bearing species, female chameleons have to descend from the branches in which they live in order to lay their eggs. This is when they are at their most vulnerable and their eggs are also often found and eaten by opportunistic predators.

LEFT A female Von Höhnel's chameleon, *Trioceros hoehnelii*, with part of a brood of young to which she gave birth a few hours previously.

their eggs under dead leaves on the forest floor. The tiger chameleon, *Calumma tigris*, from the Seychelles lays its eggs in suitable vegetation: on the island of Mahé this is introduced pineapple plants, whereas on Silhouette and Pralin they choose native species (probably endemic *Pandanus* and similar plants like palms).

Once the eggs have been laid, the female replaces the substrate and presses it down around the clutch. She may even cover the nest with twigs, leaves and other vegetation fragments. In its entirety, this may take the female a whole day. From this point onwards the female takes no further part and the young are left to fend for themselves.

There is considerable variation in the incubation period across species. In small species like *Brookesia* it is 45 to 50 days, but it can be as long as 14 to 24 months in the very large species like Parson's chameleon, *Calumma parsonii*. Other than size, the reasons for such discrepancies are not clear, but temperature and humidity evidently influence the incubation time.

Immediately after hatching, the young climb up through the substrate and emerge into the world of the forest floor. The young are perfectly capable adults in miniature and their first instinct is often to climb and begin hunting. For a few days after emerging, the young from a single clutch may remain in the vicinity and several individuals can often be found sleeping close to one another in the same bush. However, they disperse quickly after this.

Most hatchling chameleons tend to be more subdued in colour than their parents, presumably a means of reducing predation. One exception is the female Parson's

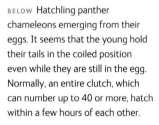

BELOW Hatchling panther chameleons emerging from their eggs. It seems that the young hold their tails in the coiled position even while they are still in the egg. Normally, an entire clutch, which can number up to 40 or more, hatch within a few hours of each other.

chameleon, *Calumma parsonii*, which is bright orange from the outset. Why this should be remains a mystery.

Baby chameleons are eating machines and growth and development is swift. Smaller species like Madagascar's montane jewel chameleon, *Furcifer campani*, reach sexual maturity in just three months, slightly larger species such as Wills' chameleon, *F. willsii*, and the lesser chameleon, *F. minor*, take four to five months, while eight months passes before the short-horned chameleon, *Calumma brevicorne*, reaches breeding condition. The largest species of all, Parson's chameleon, *C. parsonii*, does not attain sexual maturity until at least 18 months, and may take as long as three to five years.

Recent discoveries have revealed Labord's chameleon, *Furcifer labordi*, to have one of the most remarkable life histories of any reptile, with the entire generational cycle being played out in a single year. Clutches from the previous cohort lie buried until the eggs hatch in synchrony at the onset of the Malagasy rains in November. The young then develop at breakneck speed, reaching sexual maturity by January, when they pair up and mate. By late February/early March females produce and bury their eggs and then die shortly afterwards, while the eggs lay dormant until the following November when the cycle repeats. In contrast, some males outlive females, by excavating burrows at the onset of the dry season and emerging again with the next rains.

ABOVE An ephemeral chameleon. Having hatched at the onset of the rains, this newly emerged Labord's chameleon, *Furcifer labordi* will reach sexual maturity within just two months.

LEFT Several chameleon species, like this *Furcifer antimena*, inhabiting the harsh dry environments of southwest Madagascar, may have evolved an ephemeral life cycle in response to the highly seasonal fluctuations in conditions.

BELOW LEFT Labord's chameleon, *Furcifer labordi* is remarkable in that it completes its entire life cycle in a single year. Females, like this individual live for no more than three to four months.

Labord's chameleon has the shortest lifespan of any four-legged vertebrate yet studied and effectively spends a greater proportion of its 'life' as an egg (seven to eight months) than as a young/adult (four to five months). Such a life-cycle is more reminiscent of ephemeral insects and may be a strategy that has evolved in response to the extreme dry season in western Madagascar, with the chameleon channelling resources into producing larger clutches and more offspring, rather than stockpiling reserves in an attempt to make it through the dry period as an adult. It is now thought other closely related species, like *Furcifer antimena*, which live in extremely harsh seasonal environments in Madagascar may also adopt a similar strategy.

OPPOSITE The montane jewel chameleon, *Furcifer campani* from the highlands of Madagascar can reach sexual maturity in just three months.

CHAPTER 6
Chameleons and humans

PERHAPS MORE THAN ANY OTHER GROUP of lizards, chameleons have infiltrated the human psyche and become interwoven into the fabric of many indigenous customs and beliefs. Within the reptiles as a whole, only snakes command a more germane and influential cultural and mythological place.

MYTHOLOGY AND SUPERSTITION

In many areas across their range, chameleons are entwined into local folklore and superstitions, and the majority of these beliefs hold chameleons in a negative rather than positive light. For instance, in much of sub-Saharan Africa, including the island of Madagascar, chameleons are disliked or feared, and in some instances even seen as symbols of malevolence. An example from northern Ghana is typical: the belief being that if a chameleon crosses a person's path from right to left, the person must abandon their journey. Failure to do so will result in someone at the destination dying shortly after being met. In many other parts of Central and West Africa, whole chameleons and their body parts are used in local witchcraft.

The defence mechanism of African leaf chameleons, genus *Rhampholeon*, accounts for one of the most bizarre beliefs. When touched or picked up, these chameleons release tiny volumes of air and vibrate; people have likened the feeling to a slight electric shock. In Somalia, folklore would have one belief these vibrations are able to kill camels, so local herdsman are extremely wary of these completely innocuous reptiles.

In Madagascar, local beliefs and taboos known as 'fady' are central to Malagasy culture and customs across all aspects and walks of life. These vary considerably according to region and the tribal group concerned. Given that the island supports around half the world's species, it is not surprising that chameleon-based 'fady' are widespread in Madagascar.

OPPOSITE Several chameleon species thrive in peripheral habitats adjacent to human settlements. This panther chameleon, *Furcifer pardalis* is walking across the beach at a small resort on Nosy Be, north west Madagascar.

BELOW An African gold weight in the shape of a chameleon riding on the back of a snake, probably alluding to a folk tale.

In many rural areas people are simply scared of chameleons, as they believe the lizard's projectile tongue is capable of inflicting blindness. In the north, women would never handle a chameleon and, if a man accidentally comes into contact with one, his wife avoids all physical contact with her husband for at least three days.

In northeast Madagascar, the Betsimisaraka tribe consider leaf chameleons, genus *Brookesia*, to be evil spirits, calling these lizards 'ramilaheloka', which literally means 'trouble maker'. They therefore avoid touching or crossing these chameleons for fear of evil retribution. In other instances, chameleons are regarded as symbols of human character flaws and defects. People who might be regarded as untrustworthy or 'two faced', or that constantly switch their opinions, are often referred to as a 'chameleon', and this may be particularly applied to politicians.

However, not all beliefs are negative. Some Malagasy consider chameleons to be symbols of intelligence. While the lizards may be slow and physically weak, they are intellectually superior and capable of outwitting opponents and foes. In one fable – the Malagasy version of the eagle and wren – the bush pig and the chameleon disputed who was the strongest. Being much larger and more robust, the bush pig regarded the chameleon as no match. Yet, in a race, it was the chameleon that won the contest, by jumping on the pigs back at the start and leaping off its unwitting carrier at the finish. Hence, intelligence trumps physical strength.

Also, a good many Malagasy proverbs are derived from chameleon behaviour. Typical is 'Havaovy dian-tana ny fiainana, hatreo ny eo aloha ary todiho ny any afara', which literally translated means, 'Go about life the way a chameleon walks: face what is in front and look back at what lies behind'.

CONSERVATION ISSUES

Chameleons, wherever they live, are subject to both direct and indirect human pressures, which impact on their survival and have potential long-term implications for their conservation.

The main indirect pressure is habitat loss. While this is a factor that affects a huge number of species worldwide, from almost every major grouping of animals and plants, it is particularly prevalent for chameleons, as most are forest dwellers and trees are harvested perhaps more than any other living natural resource. This is exacerbated, as many species of chameleon have exact habitat requirements and consequently very restricted ranges.

In East Africa, for instance, there are approximately 40 indigenous species of chameleon, 25 of which are endemic. Many of these are isolated in 'highland islands' like the Usambara Mountains in Tanzania, and while a few species are adaptable enough to be able to survive in encroaching agricultural areas like coffee plantations, the majority cannot and perish outside native forests. The story is similar in southern Africa, where many species of dwarf chameleon, genus *Bradypodion*, have tiny natural ranges and are found only in pockets of very specific habitat like Indian Ocean coastal forest or fynbos.

The African leaf chameleons, genera *Rhampholeon* and *Rieppeleon*, which occur throughout much of Africa south of the Sahara, inhabit the leaf-litter of wet closed-canopy forests and are unable to survive beyond such habitats. Given that these forests contain the most valuable hardwoods, it is not surprising that *Rhampholeon* and *Rieppeleon* ranges are becoming increasingly restricted as specific tree harvesting and more wholesale deforestation continues to increase.

However, nowhere is the problem of habitat loss more acute than in Madagascar. The island is beset and beleaguered with environmental woes that are adversely affecting the vast majority of its endemic species, including a significant number of chameleons. Some 85 to 90% of Madagascar was once covered in forest (of many different types, according to region), a factor no doubt instrumental in over half the world's chameleon species evolving on the island. Today, however, no more than 8% of the original forest cover remains. Only a handful of species are adaptable enough to survive (even thrive) in secondary and degraded habitats; these include the panther chameleon, *Furcifer pardalis*, in the north, Oustalet's chameleon, *F. oustaleti* in the west, the warty chameleon, *F. verrucosus*, in the south and, to a much lesser extent,

BELOW Wheatfields near Caledon, South Africa, in an area that was previously covered in fynbos. It is estimated that over 90% of this unique habitat, used by several species of dwarf chameleons, *Bradypodion* sp., has been lost to agriculture and development.

the short-horned chameleon, *Calumma brevicorne* and nose-horned chameleon, *C. nasutum*, in the east. The overwhelming majority of species lack this adaptability.

Many species have extremely specific habitat requirements that restrict their natural range. Some like Parson's chameleon, *Calumma parsonii*, and the lance-nosed chameleon, *C. gallus*, appear to prefer lowland rainforests, especially along streams, whereas species like *Furcifer campani* and *C. hilleniusi* are high-altitude specialists that are restricted to isolated montane outposts. Similarly, all members of the genus *Brookesia*, the Malagasy leaf chameleons, are leaf-litter, forest-floor dwellers and inextricably tied to untouched native forests. None can survive in secondary forest. Any degradation to the habitats of these less tolerant species would ultimately result in their extinction.

Outside influences have obviously had an effect in Madagascar, with the traditional 'fady' beliefs not being taken so literally by younger generations. In many central highland areas today, young boys catch jewelled chameleons, *Furcifer lateralis*, to play with, often setting them up in opposition on a branch to fight. While such practices have a minor impact, it is undoubtedly the beginning of a slippery slope. Ecotourism in Madagascar has mushroomed over the past 20 years, with chameleons always being high on any visitors' wish list of things to see. However, finding chameleons in forests, even with the help of experienced local guides, can be frustratingly difficult. In areas adjacent to often-visited

BELOW Forest destruction in Madagascar has massively depleted the available habitat for chameleons and the vast majority of other endemic species. Slash and burn or 'tavy' cultivation is the principle culprit.

national parks and protected areas some locals have cottoned on to this and capture chameleons to subsequently 'plant' and stage 'finding' them for eager tourists. Then follows the obligatory feeding of a grasshopper to the chameleon and all in the expectation and hope of an appropriate tip. While such practices only affect a handful of individual chameleons and probably have minimal impact on overall populations, they should not be actively encouraged.

A more direct threat to chameleon survival comes from the pet trade. Given their often-spectacular appearance and fascinating behaviour, it is not surprising that chameleons create considerable interest and intrigue and demand for them in captivity has increased dramatically recently.

While a small number of species are now bred successfully in captivity (see below), the majority of species are difficult to maintain and cultivate, so are mercilessly collected from the wild. Because they are diurnal and become very pale after dark and sleep on the outer branches of vegetation, chameleons are particularly vulnerable to over-collection. Armed with nothing more than a powerful torch and a cloth sack, a skilled collector can easily devastate the populations of several species from an area in a single night. And as human nature always seems inextricably drawn to things that are rare, the demand for the more unusual and obscure species that often have very restricted natural ranges is particularly high. This is especially true in Madagascar. Being a hotbed of local endemism the illegal reptile trade is big business and rife, and

BELOW Although the native forest has largely been cleared from the central highland regions of Madagascar, in some areas small pockets of vegetation persist. Even in areas dominated by introduced species like *Eucalyptus*, some adaptable chameleons, like *Furcifer lateralis* and *Furcifer oustaleti*, can survive.

RIGHT Whereas in Africa and Madagascar many indigenous peoples fear and avoid chameleons, most visitors and wildlife enthusiasts love them. In Madagascar in particular looking for chameleons on forest walks is extremely rewarding, especially when treasures like this lovely warty chameleon, *Furcifer verrucosus*, may be found.

BELOW Many chameleons do not adapt well to captivity, and being non-social, extra stress is added when they are kept together in close confines. Unscrupulous dealers take large numbers from the wild and the chameleons suffer significant subsequent mortality.

numerous chameleon species fall victim. What is more, the survival rates of these animals once captive are pitiful, encouraging further collection from the wild. There is simply no excuse for anyone keeping wild-caught chameleons, and at all levels this should be actively discouraged.

HOW AND WHERE TO LOOK FOR CHAMELEONS

Over and above their fascinating adaptations and behaviour and often dazzling coloration, the popularity and appeal of chameleons lies in the ease with which they can be approached and observed in the wild. In general, reptiles are secretive, and most lizards in particular are shy and skittish and very difficult to watch for any length of time from close quarters. Chameleons are a spectacular exception – once found, most species can be watched from a modest distance without affecting their behaviour.

Of course in many areas in which they live, chameleons are difficult to find: after all they are primarily forest dwellers and masters of camouflage. However, there are locations where they can be found frequently and with relative ease, providing you know what you're doing.

In most localities finding chameleons during the day is challenging and most encounters are by chance. However, the dedicated chameleon watcher might spend hours systematically searching along the branches of bushes and trees in the hope of spotting something. After dark, it becomes much easier as many chameleons seek out the extremities of branches to sleep on, 'relax' their camouflaged coloration and often become pale. Furthermore, the reflective qualities of their scales are different from the surrounding foliage, making them stand out more. This makes them

BELOW Encounters during the day are more opportunistic as finding sublimely camouflaged chameleons is very challenging. The discovery of a beauty like this globe-horned chameleon, *Calumma globifer*, is a real highlight.

relatively easy to spot in a torch beam. However, it should be stressed that causing excessive disturbance to resting chameleons is unacceptable and should be avoided.

Naturally, there are other important considerations. In most places where chameleons live in Africa, for instance, there are potential hazards that need to be taken seriously. In many localities it is simply not feasible and extremely unsafe to walk in forest areas at night because of the threat from other wildlife. This not only includes the obvious large animals, but also venomous snakes. If ever there is a doubt, the advice of expert local guides should be sought. That said, searching for chameleons is feasible and safe in many places. Here are some of the renowned hot spots.

MADAGASCAR

Madagascar is undoubtedly the best place to look for chameleons not only because around half the world's species live there (and nowhere else), but also because the forests are safe to wander around in day or night (there are no large dangerous animals and no venomous snakes). Many species have particular habitat preferences and restricted ranges so can only be seen at a few specific localities. Other species are widespread and may be found in numerous places. Night walks are not allowed in many parks and reserves, but there are often adjacent areas of forest that are equally productive. Local guides are compulsory and adept at finding chameleons and other wildlife. Engaging their services will greatly enhance your experience.

ANDASIBE-MANTADIA NATIONAL PARK Certainly Madagascar's most accessible, and arguably, premier rainforest reserve. Dominated by mid-altitude montane rainforest, between 930 and 1,040 m (3051 and 3412 ft). An extensive network of paths runs through the reserve at Andasibe, while in Mantadia there are a variety of easy and more difficult trails. Opposite the main reserve is Forêt d'Analamazaotra, administered by Association Mitsinjo, which is especially good for night walks.

Frequently seen are: Parson's chameleon, *Calumma parsonii*; short-horned chameleon, *Calumma brevicorne*; stomach-striped chameleon, *Calumma gastrotaenia*; nose-horned chameleon, *Calumma nasutum* and the leaf chameleon, *Brookesia superciliaris*. Less often seen are: Malthe chameleon, *Calumma malthe*; Wills' chameleon, *Furcifer willsii* and the leaf chameleons, *Brookesia thieli* and *Brookesia therezieni*.

MASOALA NATIONAL PARK The Masoala peninsula has the largest remaining area of coastal/lowland rainforest on Madagascar. The park covers 230,000 ha (568342 acres) of largely primary forest on the western side of the peninsula and probably houses the greatest biodiversity in all of Madagascar. The forest canopy reaches over 30 m (98 ft), while the understorey is characterised by abundant palms and tree ferns with many epiphytes and orchids. This is one of the best places to see huge, spectacular turquoise-green Parson's chameleons, *Calumma parsonii*, although they are tough to find, as they tend to prefer the high understorey and forest canopy. There are comfortable lodges at Tampolo and Lohatrozona.

Frequently seen are: panther chameleon, *Furcifer pardalis*; nose-horned chameleon *Calumma nasutum*; Boettger's chameleon, *Calumma boettgeri*, and the leaf chameleon, *Brookesia superciliaris*. Less often seen are: Parson's chameleon, *Calumma parsonii* and the leaf chameleons, *Brookesia vadoni* and *Brookesia griveaudi*.

MONTAGNE D'AMBRE NATIONAL PARK An isolated patch of montane rainforest covering an area of 18,200 ha (44973 acres) between 850 m and 1,475 m (2788 and 4839 ft), Montagne d'Ambre is a green oasis in an otherwise parched landscape. The park is notable for its bird's nest ferns, tree ferns, orchids, mosses and lianas. Two waterfalls and crater lakes form focal points. This park is particularly rewarding for chameleons, including the tiny *Brookesia tuberculata*, and *B. tristis*, and other reptiles.

Frequently seen are: panther chameleon, *Furcifer pardalis*; Amber Mountain short-nosed chameleon, *Calumma amber*; Boettger's chameleon, *Calumma boettgeri*, and the leaf chameleons, *Brookesia stumpffi* and *Brookesia tuberculata*. Less often seen are: Amber Mountain chameleon, *Calumma ambreense*, and the leaf chameleon, *Brookesia antakarana*.

NOSY MANGABE RESERVE An idyllic island in the Bay of Antongil, Nosy Mangabe is cloaked in lowland rainforest and fringed with golden beaches. The canopy often exceeds 30 m (98 ft) and tree ferns, epiphytes and orchids are common. While chameleon diversity is not high, this is the best place to see Peyrieras's pygmy leaf chameleon, *Brookesia peyrierasi*, one of the world's smallest species. It is also the best place in Madagascar to see the famous leaf-tailed gecko, *Uroplatus fimbriatus*. Frequently seen are: panther chameleon, *Furcifer pardalis* and Peyrieras's pygmy leaf chameleon, *Brookesia peyrierasi*.

LEFT Nocturnal walks in Madagascar are terrific fun, and looking for and finding chameleons by torch light is hugely rewarding. Care should always be taken not to cause excessive disturbance to resting chameleons.

RANOMAFANA NATIONAL PARK This is a beautiful park covering middle and high elevation rainforest, with spectacular rivers, picturesque waterfalls, and a huge diversity of species. The area is dominated by the Namorona River, that plunges from the eastern escarpment close to the park entrance. Frequently seen are: Parson's chameleon, *Calumma parsonii*; O'Shaughnessy's chameleon, *Calumma oshaughnessyi*; blue-legged chameleon, *Calumma crypticum*; nose-horned chameleon, *Calumma nasutum* and the leaf chameleon, *Brookesia superciliaris*. Less often seen are: Glaw's chameleon, *Calumma glawi*; *Calumma fallax*; diagonal-striped chameleon, *Furcifer balteatus* and the leaf chameleon, *Brookesia nasus*.

ANKARAFANTSIKA NATIONAL PARK Ankarafantsika is one of the best remaining areas of western deciduous forest. Lac Ravelobe is a central feature and is surrounded by forest that reaches 15–20 m (49–65 ft) high. The understorey is sparse, with virtually no epiphytes but abundant lianas. A network of level paths makes walking and viewing easy. Night walks in adjacent areas are particularly rewarding. As with all western dry forest regions a greater variety of chameleons (and other reptiles) are generally visible during and after the rainy season (December–March).

Frequently seen are: Oustalet's chameleon, *Furcifer oustaleti*; rhinoceros chameleon, *Furcifer rhinoceratus* and the leaf chameleons, *Brookesia stumpffi* and *B. decaryi*. Less often seen is Angel's chameleon, *Furcifer angeli*.

ANKARANA SPECIAL RESERVE Ankarana offers a dramatic landscape of rocky outcrops, interwoven with forest. The park is dominated by impressive formations of limestone pinnacle karst or *'tsingy'*, that form an almost impenetrable fortress in places. Deciduous forest grows around periphery and penetrates into the larger canyons. Frequently seen are: Oustalet's chameleon, *Furcifer oustaleti*; panther chameleon, *Furcifer pardalis*; Petter's white-lipped chameleon, *Furcifer petteri* and the leaf chameleon, *Brookesia stumpfii*.

KIRINDY FOREST is an excellent tract of western deciduous forest growing on sandy soil and is possibly the most rewarding location in Madagascar for night walks. The canopy normally averages 12–15 m (39–49 ft), but may reach 20–25 m (65–82 ft) in the more humid areas along water courses. There is often a dense understorey and intermediate layer before the canopy. In addition there are three species of baobab, *Adansonia rubrostipa*, *A. za* and *A. grandidieri*, the latter being the largest baobab in Madagascar. Reptile and chameleon watching is at its best during and after the rains (December–March). Frequently seen are: Oustalet's chameleon, *Furcifer oustaleti* and jewelled chameleon, *Furcifer lateralis*. Less often seen are: Labord's chameleon, *Furcifer labordi*, (December to early April only), *Furcifer nicosiai* and Brygoo's leaf chameleon, *Brookesia brygooi*.

BERENTY PRIVATE RESERVE This is one of the best-known reserves in Madagascar and while Berenty is not a pristine wilderness nor is it comparable to other forest experiences in Madagascar, it offers a wealth of opportunity. Located on the banks

OPPOSITE The tiny nose-horned chameleon, *Calumma nasutum*, is extremely difficult to find during the day, but is one of the most frequently seen species on night walks in rainforest regions of Madagascar because it is numerous, turns very pale in darkness and often sleeps in low bushes.

of the Mandrare River, there are both gallery forest and spiny forest areas where chameleons can be found. Frequently seen are warty chameleon, *Furcifer verrucosus* and jewelled chameleon, *Furcifer lateralis*.

IFATY SPINY FOREST Although unprotected, the spiny forests near Ifaty are of great interest as they support a wealth of species and are some of the most bizarre forests imaginable. The forests are dominated by octopus trees, *Didierea madagascariensis* and *D. trolli*, various *Euphorbia* and *Pachypodium* species, plus two baobabs, *Adansonia rubrostipa* and *A. za*. This is the driest region on the island, with modest sporadic rainfall only between December and March. Frequently seen are warty chameleon, *Furcifer verrucosus* and *Furcifer antimena*.

EAST AFRICA

The very widespread flap-necked chameleon, *Chamaeleo dilepis*, can be encountered during the day in almost any of the major lower elevation safari destinations in Kenya and Tanzania. They are sometimes seen crossing roads and if you are 'eagle-eyed' there is a good chance you'll see occasional individuals in road-side bushes while driving along. Hotels and safaris lodges with grounds that are safe to wander around also provide plenty of opportunities to find this species. Other species that inhabit savannah areas, like the side-striped chameleon, *Chamaeleo bitaeniatus*, are much harder to see, as they are small, muted in colour and inconspicuous.

The majority of East Africa's chameleons live in upland forests that are remote and well away from the regular safari circuits. There are a few exceptions. For example, Von Höhnel's chameleon, *Trioceros hoehnelii*, can be found in the wooded suburbs of Nairobi and tourist areas like Thompson's Falls in the Aberdare Mountains, the spectacular three-horned Jackson's chameleon, *Trioceros jacksonii*, is also seen in Nairobi's wooded suburbs, while the Ruwenzori side-striped chameleon, *Chamaeleo rudis*, can be seen in the grounds of the safari lodges around the rim of the Ngorongoro Crater in Tanzania.

SOUTHERN AFRICA

The flap-necked chameleon, *Chamaeleo dilepis*, is also widespread in southern Africa and is regularly seen on safaris in the region. Visitors to the spectacular arid areas and coastal dunes of Namibia have a good chance of seeing the Namaqua chameleon, *Chamaeleo namaquensis*, either on low lying bushes, walking across open ground or standing erect on a rock to fine-tune its body temperature, the latter being unlike the behaviour of any other chameleon.

OTHER AREAS

Elsewhere, chameleons are very difficult to see. In the Mediterranean region, India and Sri Lanka, for example, they are rare and, unless you are very fortunate, or have expert local help, the chances of finding a colony are slim. Likewise, the Arabian species live in areas where casual nature-watching is difficult and sometimes ill-advised.

CHAMELEONS AS PETS

Chameleons' colourful appearance, intriguing behaviour, deliberate gait and non-aggressive disposition have captured the public imagination, with increased demand resulting in them becoming a significant factor in the reptile pet trade. Unfortunately, they are not easy to look after and can only be recommended to those who have already had some success with other species of lizards. These notes are not intended as a comprehensive guide to maintaining chameleons in captivity but rather to highlight some of the pitfalls and to illustrate the commitment necessary if they are to be kept properly. Anyone unable to provide the necessary conditions should not consider keeping chameleons.

The most easily obtained species are the veiled chameleon, *Chamaeleo calyptratus*, and the panther chameleon, *Furcifer pardalis*, both of which are bred in captivity by a number of dedicated amateur herpetologists. Only captive-bred animals should be considered: chameleon populations are under threat in many parts of the world and trade in them only increases the pressure on wild stocks. In any case, captive-bred individuals will be free of disease and parasites, and will have better temperaments than wild ones. Furthermore, the breeder or supplier should be able to provide basic instructions on how the parents are kept, including information on their environment and diet, and this will provide a starting point for the correct care of the offspring.

BELOW The veiled chameleon, *Chamaeleo calyptratus*, is an adaptable species that fares well, and can be bred in large numbers, under captive conditions.

Some generalisations can be made. The large, showy species, which are the most popular ones, are highly visual and territorial reptiles. Males cannot be kept together in the same cage and females sometimes become stressed if they are housed communally; even animals housed separately can become stressed if they are able to see other chameleons in nearby cages. Cages should be large and well ventilated and contain plenty of branches or vines for climbing on, and dense vegetation, either natural or artificial, so that the animals can remain hidden. Spraying on a daily basis is important as chameleons are reluctant to drink from a bowl and, in addition, some species require humid conditions, in keeping with their natural habitats. The best cages are those made entirely from metal mesh and their size should be commensurate with that of the chameleon species – some, such as the popular panther chameleon, require cages measuring at least 1.5 m (5 ft) in every direction once they become adult.

Unless the chameleons are kept outdoors, which is unlikely, they will lack Vitamin D, which is necessary to synthesise calcium. The natural source of this vitamin

BELOW The panther chameleon, in all its regional forms, is popular with reptile-keepers and, given enough attention and expertise, will thrive and breed in captivity. This form is from the Ambilobe region, in the far north of Madagascar.

is sunlight, but it can be provided artificially by ultraviolet lighting in the form of a UV-B lamp, preferably one developed specifically for reptiles. As the output of these varies from one manufacturer to another it is not possible to give the distance from the chameleon, nor the length of time they should be left on for; advice must be sought from the supplier. Supplementary heating, in the form of background heating or a spotlight, may also be necessary, again depending on the species concerned and your location. This is in addition to the UV lamp, which does not give out a significant amount of heat.

Healthy chameleons have huge appetites and require a constant supply of food in the form of insects. The staple foods for insectivorous reptiles are crickets and locusts, which are available from specialist suppliers or by mail order. These should be dusted with a dietary supplement formulated specifically for reptiles before they are offered to the chameleons, as a monotonous diet of cultured food is invariably lacking in essential minerals and vitamins. Under some circumstances, wild-caught insects such as grasshoppers may be used to provide a change in diet.

CHAPTER 7
Chameleon genera

THIS CHAPTER IS AN OVERVIEW of the ten genera of chameleons, describing their distinguishing features, distribution and natural history. Additional information is given on some of the characteristic or notable species in each genus. The three genera of leaf or pygmy chameleons currently placed within the subfamily Brookesiinae are dealt with first, followed by the seven genera of Chamaeleoninae.

OPPOSITE There are 26 species of Malagasy leaf chameleons, genus *Brookesia*, all of which are endemic forest floor dwellers. Most species inhabit the eastern rainforests. *Brookesia nasus* prefers higher elevation forests. This individual is from Ranomafana National Park.

BROOKESIA (MADAGASCAN PYGMY OR LEAF CHAMELEONS)

There are 31 species of *Brookesia*, all small, brown chameleons resembling dead leaves or, in a few cases, decorated with frills and flaps to resemble mosses and lichens. Their tails are short and stiff, and not prehensile. They are mostly ground dwellers in the day but climb into low bushes and ferns, etc. at night. The two smallest species of chameleons, *B. micra* and *B. minima*, are included in this genus. Females are larger than males and they are all egg-layers as far as is known. The genus is named for the nineteenth-century zoologist Joshua Brookes, about whom little appears to be known.

LEFT The leaf chameleon, *Brookesia thieli*, is particularly slender and unlike many congeners, does not have a dorsal ridge.

RIGHT *Brookesia superciliaris* is one of the most widespread leaf chameleon species in Madagascar. This individual is from Masoala National Park in north east Madagascar.

RIGHT *Brookesia superciliaris* is one of the most widespread leaf chameleon species in Madagascar. This individual is from Masoala National Park in north east Madagascar.

BELOW The Antsingy leaf chameleon, *Brookesia perarmata*, is the largest *Brookesia* species and is known only from the Tsingy de Bemaraha area in western Madagascar. It is endangered and consequently highly sought after in the illegal pet trade.

The recently named *Brookesia micra* is now regarded as the world's smallest chameleon, perhaps the smallest of all reptiles, with females measuring up to 30 mm (1¼ in) and males even smaller. It occurs in northern Madagascar and belongs to a group of fifteen very similar chameleons, some of which, such as *B. minima* and *B. tuberculata*, are almost as small. Several species are poorly known and four have only recently been described. Some species have tiny ranges, just a square kilometre in one case. They are all brown in colour, often paler above than below and with no definite markings. Their bodies are slender and their legs very thin. In at least some species the males 'guard' the slightly larger females by mounting their backs and being carried around for several days until mating takes place. Their eggs are extremely small, measuring about 25 x 15 mm (about ¹⁄₁₀ x ¹⁄₁₅ in). This is roughly the size of a grain of rice.

Brookesia superciliaris is among the most widespread of the pygmy chameleons, and is found in rainforests throughout the eastern half of Madagascar. Its most distinguishing feature is the pair of raised 'eyebrows', which give it its scientific name. It is a ground-dwelling species that climbs into low vegetation to roost at night, to avoid predators such as snakes. It typically sleeps at the tips of thin branches or leaves so that any attempt to creep up on it will disturb the twig, causing the chameleon to drop to the ground.

The Antsingy leaf chameleon, *Brookesia perarmata*, is one of the most unusual species. It is larger than most leaf chameleons, growing to 11 cm (just under 4½ in), has raised 'eyebrows' like those of *B. superciliaris*, and a frilled structure extends from the back of its head to cover the nape of its neck. There is a row of flattened spines along each side of its backbone and an additional series of conical structures, formed from clusters of keeled scales, along the flanks. Its head is usually yellow or tan

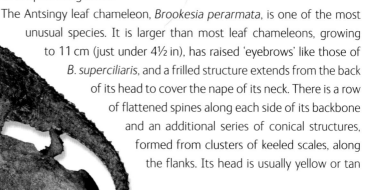

and the body rich brown. This species is restricted to a small area in the west of Madagascar, the Tsingy de Bemaraha, and its entire range apparently falls within the nature reserve of the same name. The only other Madagascan leaf chameleon that approaches *B. perarmata* in appearance is *B. ebenaui*, which occurs only on the northern tip of the island, in the region around Diego Suarez.

Brygoo's pygmy chameleon, *Brookesia brygooi*, is another species with pointed conical structures over each eye. It lacks a dorsal ridge but has a series of spines along each side of the back. It is brown and tan, often lighter on the back than the flanks and it is particularly well camouflaged when resting among dead leaves. This species pretends to be dead if threatened, closing its eyes and lying motionless on its side. It is from the dry deciduous forests of western Madagascar, whereas most *Brookesia* are from humid forests in the east, and, in particular, its range does not overlap that of *B. superciliaris*, which is probably its closest relative.

RHAMPHOLEON (AFRICAN LEAF CHAMELEONS)

Fourteen species of small chameleons from East and West Africa are placed in the genus *Rhampholeon*. The name of the genus is derived from the Greek words 'rhampho', meaning beaked and 'leon', meaning lion, the name 'beaked-lion' referring to the pointed snout of some species. The genus as a whole occurs in a broad swathe from eastern Nigeria to the East African coast in Tanzania.

They range from about 5 to 10 cm (2 to 4 in) in length and are mostly some shade of brown or buff in colour, the exception being *Rhampholeon viridis*, males of which are green. Most lack any bold markings, although several species have faint stripes and blotches on their flanks. Most African leaf chameleons have short, non-prehensile tails, although some species do use their tails to brace themselves when climbing. Some are deep-bodied, others less so. Males of several species have soft

BELOW The West African leaf chameleon, *Rhampholeon spectrum*, a wide-ranging West African member of the genus.

'horns' at the tip of their snouts and males are often significantly smaller than females, sometimes less than half their total length. They are diurnal, climbing into low bushes at night to sleep and, in their general appearance and behaviour, they closely parallel the *Brookesia* species from Madagascar. They are all egg-layers as far as is known, although at least one species, Marshall's pygmy chameleon, *R. marshalli*, lays eggs that already contain well-developed embryos when laid and which hatch after a short incubation period. African leaf chameleons are reported to vibrate violently when picked up, producing a buzzing sensation which is thought to startle predators into dropping them.

Several species occur in Tanzania and in the Democratic Republic of the Congo, where they are each restricted to small pockets of isolated rainforests, and where deforestation is a threat to their survival. Others, however, such as the west African leaf chameleon, *Rhampholeon spectrum*, which hails from Cameroon and neighbouring countries in West Africa, are more widely distributed. The latter species is pale brown or reddish-brown in colour and lacks any well-defined markings. It occurs in dense rainforests, and, like the other members of the genus and also the Madagascan leaf chameleons, it spends its days among the leaf-litter and climbs into low vegetation at night.

ABOVE The pygmy grass chameleon, *Rieppeleon kerstenii*, closely resembles many Malagasy leaf chameleons, genus *Brookesia*. This individual was photographed in the Sokoke Forest on the Kenyan coast.

RIEPPELEON (SHORT-TAILED CHAMELEONS)

This genus contains three species of small, brown chameleons from East Africa that were included in *Rhampholeon* until 2004 when the new genus was erected on the basis of certain structural features of their skull. All three species are fairly wide-ranging in East Africa and are not restricted to isolated mountain ranges. In other respects, though, their lifestyle is similar to that of the *Rhampholeon* species and they are all egg-layers as far as is known. They are named for the leading herpetologist Olivier Rieppel.

The short-tailed chameleon, *Rieppeleon brevicaudatus*, occurs in Tanzania and southern Kenya and grows to just over 9 cm (3 ½ in). Males have proportionately longer tails and their eye turrets are greenish. Females are uniform pale brown. The pygmy grass chameleon, *R. kerstenii*, is also from Tanzania and Kenya and this species has a more slender body shape than the previous species and, in this respect, it closely resembles some of the *Brookesia* species such as *B. minima* (which is, however, much smaller).

OPPOSITE The short-tailed dwarf chameleon, *Rieppeleon brevicaudatus*, occurs in the Eastern Arc Mountains of Tanzania. It is sometimes called the bearded dwarf chameleon due to the two or three elongated scales on its chin.

BRADYPODION (SOUTH AFRICAN LEAF CHAMELEONS)

At present, there are 17 species of *Bradypodion*, many having been described in the last 30 years, with others currently awaiting description. The members of this interesting genus are endemic to South Africa and neighbouring Namibia and Lesotho. Their name is derived from two Greek words, 'brady', meaning slow, and 'podi', meaning feet, in reference to their slow and deliberate gait. They are small chameleons, growing to a maximum of 15 cm (6 in), but most are smaller than this. Many are brightly coloured, often green, but sometimes having large areas of bluish, yellow or orange scales. A few species are more cryptically coloured in browns and greys. Most have enlarged, stud-like scales scattered randomly on their flanks and they have a low crest of tooth-like or conical scales running down their back, and sometimes extending onto their tail. Most have a 'beard' of enlarged gular scales on their chin and throat. Both sexes lack horns or other nose appendages but they have a bony crest or casque at the nape of their neck.

Dwarf chameleons live in a variety of habitats. Several species, such as the Knysna dwarf chameleon, *Bradypodion damaranum*, and the Natal Midlands dwarf chameleon, *B. thamnobates*, live in closed-canopy forests, sometimes high up in trees, although they occasionally venture into adjacent grasslands and bushes. Another group of species, including the Little Karoo dwarf chameleon, *B. gutterale*, occur in the fynbos vegetation, which consists of fine-leaved bushes and clumps of the grass-like restios plants, while the western dwarf chameleon, *B. occidentale*, can be found in the drier dune vegetation along the west coast of South Africa. All the species are live-bearers, giving birth to 5 to 15 young after a gestation period of about three months.

Bradypodion pumilum, the Cape dwarf chameleon, first described in 1802, is probably the best-known species due to its occurrence in the vicinity of Cape Town, where it lives in gardens and parks as well as more natural environments such as fynbos and renosterveld. It is highly variable but is usually some shade of green with irregular stripes along its flanks. There is some correlation between habitat types and pattern, with the 'typical' form, from gardens, forests and bushes, being the most brightly coloured and the fynbos and renosterveld forms being smaller and less colourful. This is one of the more adaptable species. Others, however, are restricted to small isolated remnant forest patches and as a result their ranges are very small.

CALUMMA

This genus consists of 32 species of medium-sized to large, brightly coloured, arboreal chameleons from Madagascar and nearby islands (including the Seychelles). All have long, prehensile tails. Males are larger than females and often have horns or crests. Both sexes may have occipital lobes or flaps and it is this feature that most easily distinguishes them from the other genus of large, brightly coloured Malagasy chameleons, *Furcifer*. They occur in the humid forests of eastern and central Madagascar. All species are egg-layers as far as is known. The word *Calumma* comes from the Greek 'kalymma' meaning a veil but also used to describe the gills of fish. The lobes of several of the members of this genus are indeed reminiscent of fishes' gill-flaps.

The short-horned chameleon, *Calumma brevicorne*, also known as the elephant-eared chameleon, shows the characteristic occipital lobes to good effect. In this species the nasal horn is short in males, and almost absent in females. This is a large species in which males can grow to 40.5 cm (16 in), females being significantly smaller, and it occurs in a variety of colours, mostly greys and browns, with a reddish nose-horn. The blue-legged chameleon, *C. crypticum*, is closely related but more widespread over the eastern half of Madagascar: in the past these two species, and possibly others, were confused.

Parson's chameleon, *Calumma parsonii*, is the largest species in the genus and, by most measures, the largest chameleon (although Oustalet's chameleon, *Furcifer oustaleti*, sometimes grows longer it is a more slender species). Males can grow to 69.5 cm (about 27 in), females to 49.5 cm (about 19 ½ in) and it is a bulky, deep-bodied species. In males, the snout is adorned with a pair of short, bony horns and there is a bony casque reaching back over the neck. The neck

BELOW The short-horned chameleon, *Calumma brevicorne*, is also known as the elephant-eared chameleon, because of its large occipital lobes.

flaps are greatly reduced. It is typically blue-green or turquoise in colour but yellow individuals also occur. Parson's chameleon has a wide range in the east of Madagascar and probably occurs in all areas with lowland rainforests, where it is more likely to occur in open forest, forest edges and near streams than in the most densely wooded areas. Due to its size, this chameleon can tackle large prey including small vertebrates such as other lizards and small mammals, although it is not known if these form a significant part of its diet in the wild. O'Shaughnessy's chameleon, *C. oshaughnessyi*, and the globe-horned chameleon, *C. globifer*, are similar but smaller.

RIGHT Only adult male blue-legged chameleons, *Calumma crypticum*, develop the spectacular coloration that gives the species its name.

BELOW O'Shaughnessy's chameleon, *Calumma oshaughnessyi*, is a species from central eastern and south eastern regions of Madagascar.

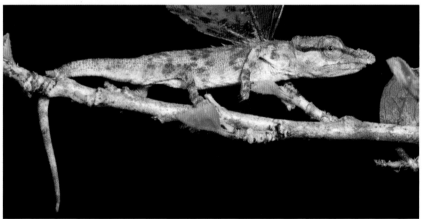

ABOVE The nose-horned chameleon, *Calumma nasutum*, is probably the smallest of the 'true' chameleons, subfamily Chamaeleoninae.

LEFT *Calumma fallax* is a very similar in appearance to *C. nasutum*, but has a distinctive line of dorsal spines.

Of the smaller species in the genus, the nose-horned chameleon, *Calumma nasutum*, is the most common, occurring throughout the more humid forests of the east, and frequently seen in low vegetation at the sides of roads and tracks, as well as in the understorey of primary rainforests. Its 'horn' is actually a soft, fleshy appendage covered in small scales, and is present in both sexes. It is usually brown or reddish-brown in colour although some individuals are more colourful. *C. fallax*, *C. boettgeri* and *C. guibei* are similar and, furthermore, it is possible that *C. 'nasutum'* is actually a complex of more than one species.

The forked chameleon, *Calumma furcifer*, is a rare species only known from a limited area in eastern Madagascar. Males are unique in having a nasal appendage that has a short trunk which divides into two, like a letter Y. This makes them instantly recognizable, but females lack the horn and are similar to several other species. Guibe's chameleon, *C. guibei*, and the blade chameleon, *C. gallus*, are notable for their very long, but undivided, horns and the fact that females also have horns, though not as long as those of males. Boettger's chameleon, *C. boettgeri*, from northern Madagascar has a shorter nasal appendage which may be bright blue in parts of its range. This species, as presently understood, may turn out to be two or more species owing to the great variation in coloration and the shape of the nasal appendage.

Two species, *C. glawi* and *C. vencesi*, described in 1997 and 2001 respectively, are named in honour of Frank Glaw and Miguel Vences, who have been instrumental in increasing our knowledge of, and interest in, the amphibians and reptiles of Madagascar by producing the first (and only) comprehensive field guide to the region, as well as describing nearly 100 new species from the region.

CHAMAELEO (TYPICAL CHAMELEONS)

Seventeen species of medium-sized to large chameleons, wide-ranging in Africa, the Mediterranean region of Europe, the Middle East, India and Sri Lanka, are placed in the genus *Chamaeleo*. There is an additional species, *C. monachus*, on the island of Socotra, situated off the Horn of Africa but politically part of South Yemen. Many of the species previously included in this genus were recently moved to a different genus, *Trioceros*. Most *Chamaeleo* species are arboreal but some are very adaptable and may live in low vegetation or even on the ground. They display a range of colours but are often green or greenish, with the ability to change colour rapidly in response to a variety of stimuli. None of the *Chamaeleo* species have nasal horns or appendages although several species have raised, helmet-like casques on the top of their heads. Several have flaps covering their necks and one, the Namaqua chameleon, *C. namaquensis*, has a dorsal crest consisting of a series of angular knobs. All the species are egg-layers as far as is known. The name of the genus, and indeed all chameleons, is derived from two Greek words: 'khamai', which means dwarf, and 'leon', which means lion. So chameleon ('khamaileon' in Greek) means 'dwarf lion', probably referring to their ferocity when cornered or when fighting among themselves.

The veiled chameleon, *Chamaeleo calyptratus*, is an unusual species from the Arabian Peninsula, occurring in Yemen and southwest Saudi Arabia. It is most common on the heavily cultivated south and west-facing mountain slopes that capture rain from the humid winds originating over the Indian Ocean and the Red Sea. Some populations live on the drier coastal plain, especially in the neighbourhood of wadis and streams, and on the dry, cool highland plateau, where temperatures can fall to freezing point at night. They may be unique among chameleons by including a small amount of plant material, mostly leaves, in their diet (although there is some evidence that the Namaqua chameleon, *C. namaquensis,* and Jackson's chameleon, *Trioceros jacksonii*, will also eat leaves). Males sometimes grow to 60 cm (24 in) in total length although most are about 45 cm (about 18 in). Females rarely grow more than 30 cm (12 in) in total length. Both sexes are green or greenish-blue in colour, with wide transverse bands of yellow, tan or buff but, in keeping with most chameleons, coloration is extremely variable and males tend to be more brightly coloured than females. Males also have a much higher casque than females. Gravid females become dark green or black with scattered spots of blue and yellow. This species regularly breeds in captivity and is very prolific: females may produce three clutches of up to 70 eggs each year. They are short-lived, however, and rarely survive to breed for a second season. Captive veiled chameleons become tame and make interesting pets as long as the correct conditions are provided.

The Mediterranean chameleon, *Chamaeleo chamaeleon*, is the original chameleon, named by Linnaeus (as *Lacerta chamaeleon*) in his *Systema naturæ* in 1758. It is the only species to occur in Europe, in southern Greece, Spain, Portugal, Cyprus and Malta, and has an extensive range in North Africa, the Middle East and the Arabian Peninsula. It grows to about 24 cm (9 ½ in) and females are slightly larger than males on average. This is not one of the most brightly coloured species, being overall brown or olive, with the ability to darken to black and lighten to pale green or yellowish. There are spots and blotches superimposed on these colours including a series of pale spots along the flanks, sometimes joined to form a line, and light-coloured bars along the dorsal crest. They live in trees and shrubs, including Mediterranean species of oaks, pines, junipers and heathers. Females bury their clutches of 5 to about 45 eggs and these take ten months to a year to hatch under natural conditions.

BELOW This Ruwenzori side-striped chameleon, *Chamaeleo rudis*, from the montane forests on the rim of the Ngorongoro Crater, Tanzania, is typical of many of the smaller *Chamaeleo* species in the east African highlands.

ABOVE The Namaqua chameleon, *Chamaeleo namaquensis*, is atypical of chameleons in so many ways, being largely terrestrial and inhabiting arid desert regions.

The Namaqua chameleon, *Chamaeleo namaquensis*, is a species that appears to have lost its way; it has all the typical chameleon adaptations for an arboreal lifestyle but lives in the treeless deserts of Namibia, South Africa and extreme southern Angola. It is a large species, growing to 25 cm (10 in), and has a short tail. It has a bony casque on top of its head and a crest made up of almost square-shaped knobs. It is brown, olive-green or buff in colour, with a row of paler blotches down its flanks and is covered overall with small scattered dark spots. This unusual chameleon lives in the gravelly inter-dune plains of the Namib Desert and the South African Karoo, sometimes resting in shrubby plants but often found many miles from the nearest vegetation. It feeds on tenebrionid beetles which also live among the dunes and which are famous for their habit of collecting water by taking up positions along the dune ridges when moist fogs roll in from the Atlantic. It is likely that the chameleons obtain nearly all of their water from their food: they are effective hunters and rarely miss an opportunity to feed. Little is known about their habits and life-cycle. Populations within striking distance of large towns are being adversely affected by the use of recreational off-road vehicles.

The African flap-necked chameleon, *Chamaeleo dilepis*, is probably the most widespread of all chameleons and is a familiar lizard over much of Africa south of the Sahara. It occurs from Cameroon in the west to Ethiopia in the east, and as far south as the Northern Cape region of South Africa. As its common name implies, it is characterised by a casque that extends back to form a pair of flaps on its neck, although this feature is also found in other chameleons. Its colour and morphology vary throughout its range and at least three forms are recognised, sometimes as subspecies. Variation occurs in the colour of the interstitial skin of its chin, for instance, which it displays when it puffs out its throat, and this skin may be orange, yellow or grey. This chameleon is commonly seen on the ground, crossing roads and tracks, and climbing into small shrubs such as acacia, but it may also climb into taller trees. In parts of its range this species avoids cold and dry conditions by hiding in burrows or holes in trees and becoming inactive.

OPPOSITE The flap-necked chameleon, *Chamaeleo dilepis*, is widespread in the savannah bushlands of east and southern Africa.

FURCIFER

The genus *Furcifer* consists of 20 medium-sized to large species. Eighteen of them are endemic to Madagascar and two, *F. cephalolepis* and *F. polleni*, to the Comoros Islands. One species, the panther chameleon, *F. pardalis*, also occurs on the island of Réunion in the Indian Ocean, where it is presumed to have been introduced. Male *Furcifer* are much larger than females and often have horns and other nasal appendages. A bony ridge is always present over the top of the head, starting roughly in line with the eyes and becoming higher towards the back of the head. Although this is present in both sexes it is more pronounced in males. The *Furcifer* species tend to live in drier habitats than *Calumma* species, and have a more western and southern distribution on Madagascar, although the panther chameleon occurs in the north and northeast while the jewelled chameleon, *F. lateralis*, and Oustalet's chameleon, *F. oustaleti*, occur in the east and the central highlands as well as the west. Some species, notably *F. lateralis*, are common in parks and gardens but most occur in dry deciduous forests. All species are egg-layers as far as is known. The generic name *Furcifer* relates to the forked (i.e. furcate or bifurcate) horns borne by some members of the genus.

Male panther chameleons may grow to over 50 cm (about 20 in) in total length and females to 37 cm (14 ½ in). Both sexes have long, prehensile tails, typically as long as, or slightly longer than, their snout-vent length. The coloration in this species is extremely variable and many forms are recognised. The panther chameleon occurs in a range of habitats, often in large numbers, in the north and northwest of Madagascar, in addition to the introduced population on Réunion. Its adaptability has made it popular among amateur reptile keepers and breeders as it will thrive under a wide range of conditions. In addition, there are many colour forms corresponding

OPPOSITE Male warty chameleons, *Furcifer verrucosus*, are relatively large, but are still able to carefully pick their way through tangles of thorns in the spiny forest of southern Madagascar.

BELOW Most *Furcifer* species inhabit the drier western and southern regions of Madagascar. One exception is diagonal-striped chameleon, *Furcifer balteatus*, which lives in eastern rainforests. This one is from Ranomafana National Park.

The rhinoceros chameleon, *Furcifer rhinoceratus*, is restricted to dry deciduous forests in north west Madagascar.

Petter's chameleon, *Furcifer petteri*, inhabits dry forests in the far north of Madagascar.

with distinct geographic localities, such as the mainly blue forms from the islands of Nosy Faly and Nosy Be, and the bright green and red form from Nosy Mangabe and neighbouring parts of the mainland. Its natural habitat is rainforests but it also occurs in large numbers in plantations, gardens and roadside hedges. Females lay up to 46 eggs, which they bury in sandy soil. These may take more than one year to hatch although the incubation period is shortened to about five months under constant warm conditions.

Oustalet's chameleon, *Furcifer oustaleti*, is a large, common species, growing to 68.5 cm (27 in) in length. Males are often dull grey or brown in colour but females may have areas of pink or orange on their bodies, and in some regions they are green. Like the jewelled chameleon, this species has adapted to urban habitats and can even be seen walking across dirt yards and on garden walls. This species is very prolific, with clutches of over 60 eggs having been recorded. The warty chameleon, *F. verrucosus*, is similar but has a dorsal crest that is more spiny than that of Oustalet's chameleon and a row of tubercles along its flanks. It is found throughout the drier parts of Madagascar and is especially common in the far south.

The jewelled chameleon, *Furcifer lateralis*, is one of the smaller species of *Furcifer*, with males growing to almost 30 cm (12 in) in total length and females to 22 cm (8 ½ in). Males' tails account for more than half their total length but in females they are relatively shorter. Males are usually bright emerald green whereas females are more variable and may be brown, yellowish or green. There is invariably a white stripe running along the flanks, often with three darker circles superimposed upon it. Jewelled chameleons live in a variety of habitats, including forests and open grasslands, and are especially common in parks and gardens even within the capital city of Antananarivo, for instance. Females lay up to about 20 eggs, which hatch after five months to a year. The babies grow rapidly, reaching maturity in less than six months.

LEFT A male Labord's chameleon, *Furcifer labordi*, notable for its nasal appendage, high casque and short lifespan.

ABOVE Male forked chameleons, *Furcifer bifidus*, have a pair of prominent appendages on their snout but these are absent in females. This species occurs in the humid coastal forests of eastern Madagascar.

Although males of many *Furcifer* species, including all those mentioned so far, have only rudimentary nasal protuberances, several others are well-endowed in this respect. The aptly-named rhinoceros chameleon, *F. rhinoceratus*, has a single horn, flattened from side to side and slightly upturned, and the female has a smaller version. This species is from northwestern Madagascar, and lives in dry deciduous forests. Other species, such as the white-lined chameleon, *F. antimena*, Labord's chameleon, *F. labordi*, and Angel's chameleon, *F. angeli*, also have single rigid horns whereas Petter's chameleon, *F. petteri*, the two-horned chameleon, *F. bifidus*, lesser chameleon, *F. minor*, Wills, chameleon, *F. willsii* and the diagonal-striped chameleon, *F. balteatus*, all have paired appendages. Some of these, including the latter two species, are unusual in that they occur in dry regions. In all these species males are significantly larger than females, in some case twice their length and, therefore, considerably more than twice their weight. *Furcifer labordi* is known for its very short lifespan, growing to maturity in less than three months, and living only for a single season. Similar species, such as *F. antimena*, may have similarly rapid turnovers.

BELOW A young warty chameleon, *Furcifer verrucosus*, from the dry southern part of Madagascar.

ABOVE A male Böhme's two-horned chamaeleon, *Kinyongia boehmei*, from Kenya.

KINYONGIA

This is a new genus described in 2006 and containing 17 species from East Africa, previously placed in *Bradypodion* or *Chamaeleo*. They may be small or large, and bright or dull in coloration, but all are arboreal species. Males of some species have horns, bony casques on top of their heads, or both, whereas others lack ornamentation. Horned species may have a single flattened horn or a pair of flattened horns and they are sometimes known collectively as blade-horned chameleons. Some species have small ranges and are poorly known: a number of new species have been described recently and their relationships and identification can be difficult. The genus includes egg-laying as well as live-bearing species, with the live-bearers occurring mainly at high elevations. *Kinyongia* is derived from the Swahili word for chameleon, 'kinyonga'.

Fischer's chameleon, also known as the Nguru blade-horned chameleon, *Kinyongia fischeri*, is a medium-sized species growing to just over 20cm (8in). This chameleon is restricted to a few localities within the Nguru Mountains, in eastern Tanzania. Confusingly, several other species of chameleons from the region, which also have the characteristically paired nasal appendages, were formerly included under the *fischeri* 'umbrella' illustrating the difficulties in separating species that look superficially similar but which are genetically distinct. True *K. fischeri* is only known from a small number of specimens. By contrast, the Rwenzori plate-nosed chameleon, *K. xenorhina*, is unmistakable. In addition to its large, flattened horn it also has a raised casque of roughly the same size, so that the head has a shape that has been likened by Colin Tilbury, an expert on African chameleons, to a wing nut.

NADZIKAMBIA

This new genus, which was described in 2006, contains two species at present. They are the Mount Mlanje chameleon, *Nadzikambia mlanjense*, from Malawi, and *N. baylissi*, only described in 2010 and found in Mozambique. *N. mlanjense* was previously placed in *Chamaeleo* and then *Bradypodion* but the two species appear not to be closely related to other chameleons. They are thought to be egg-layers. The genus gets its name from the word for chameleon, 'nadzikambe', in the ChiChewa language of the people who live in the area where *N. mlanjense* was first discovered. The two species have no nose horns or other features that distinguish them from members of the *Chamaeleo* genus but have been separated on the basis of the structure of their hemipenes and cellular differences.

TRIOCEROS

Thirty-nine species are included in this newly erected genus, containing species formerly included within *Chamaeleo*. They are arboreal chameleons, usually green in colour and several range from Togo in West Africa to the East African coasts of Kenya and Tanzania. *Trioceros* means 'three-horned', which is rather unfortunate since, although the best-known species, *T. jacksonii*, and some other species, do indeed have three horns, most of the remaining species do not. Some have two or four horns, while others have no horns at all. A small number of species from West Africa, have a high dorsal ridge, or 'sailfin'.

Jackson's chameleon, *Trioceros jacksonii*, is the archetypal species in this genus. It is often likened to a miniature *Triceratops*, owing to the three long horns attached to the snouts of males. They use their horns in combat, interlocking with each other and attempting to dislodge their rival from the branch. The horns of the females are sometimes absent altogether but are more often reduced to small bony tubercles on the snout. Males grow to 26 cm (10 ¼ in) in length, females are significantly smaller. The species is usually green or yellowish-green in colour, but there are local variations. The Mount Meru three-horned chameleon, *Trioceros jacksonii merumontanus*, for example, as well as being smaller than the typical form, has blue-green eyeballs and a yellow dorsal crest. The bony ridges on its head are also yellow, making this one of the more colourful chameleons in Africa. This species is viviparous, giving birth

BELOW A particularly brightly coloured male Von Höhnel's chameleon, *Trioceros hoehnelii*, from Kenya.

LEFT A female crested chameleon, *Trioceros cristatus*. Compared to the male on page 6, for instance, the female is coloured differently and the dorsal crest is less developed.

to about 20 young, although litters of up to 82 have been recorded. The gestation period is thought to be about ten months and the young reach maturity when they are about nine months old.

Despite lacking horns, the crested chameleon, *Trioceros cristatus*, from West Africa is one of the more impressive species because of the large dorsal crest of the males. Females also have crests, but they are lower. Males of this species are predominantly orange whereas females are green, although both are changeable to some degree. They live in low vegetation in lowland and coastal rainforests. This species is oviparous, laying between 16 and 37 eggs. Several other chameleons from the same region, notably the Cameroon two-horned mountain chameleon, *T. montium*, are similar although in this species the crest on the back is lower whereas that on the tail is higher. As far as is known, this group of West African species all lay eggs.

Von Höhnel's chameleon (sometimes called the Kenyan high-casqued chameleon), *T. hoehnelii*, is an East African species, found in the highlands of Kenya and on Mount Elgon, in Uganda. It is a relatively small species but males, in particular, are very colourful, being green or blue. Females are more likely to be yellowish-green or olive, but there is variation in both sexes, depending to some extent on their origin. The species is easily recognised by its bony casque, which is relatively large, and an upturned snout ending in a small horn made up of several tubercles. This species is very tolerant of cold and lives in areas that often drop below freezing point. They are very common in places and local boys often catch them and place them on sticks to offer to tourists for the purpose of having their photograph taken. This species is viviparous, giving birth to around ten young. Viviparity in reptiles is often an adaptation to life in cool climates, where the female's ability to raise her temperature by moving around and basking gives them the ability to speed up the progress of their developing young.

Index

Credits and further information

PICTURE CREDITS

3, 4, 5, 6, 8, 9, 11, 12, 14, 16, 17, 20 below, 21, 22 below, 24, 25 left, 26 below, 28, 29, 30, 36, 38, 42 below, 46/47, 53, 60, 61, 64, 65, 66/67, 68, 71 below, 73, 75, 77, 85, 86/87, 91, 93, 94, 95, 97 above, 105 left, 105 below, 106, 106/107, 108, 109 © Chris Mattison
7, 10, 13, 15, 18, 19, 20 right, 23, 25 below, 26 right, 27, 31, 32, 32-33, 34, 35, 37, 39, 41, 42 right, 43, 44, 45, 48/49, 50, 51, 52, 54, 58, 59, 63, 69, 70, 71 left, 72, 76, 78, 79, 81, 82, 88, 89, 90, 92, 96, 97 left, 99, 100, 101, 102, 103, 104, 105 above © Nick Garbutt
22 right © Christopher V. Anderson, 40 NHPA/Anthony Bannister, 55 © Wikipedia, 56 © Edwin Giesbers/naturepl.com, 62 © Pete Oxford/naturepl.com, 67 above © Biosphoto/ Daniel Heuclin

AUTHOR'S ACKNOWLEDGEMENTS

Chris Mattison would like to thank the people who have helped him find and photograph chameleons in the field or in captivity: Ben Cornick, Jeremy Fletcher, Toby Mace, Ben Middleton, John Pickett, Anslem de Silva, Wharf Aquatics, and several guides in Madagascar, all of whose help was invaluable and greatly appreciated.

Nick Garbutt would like to thank the numerous guides in Madagascar who have helped him find chameleons all over the island. In particular special thanks extend to Hery Andrianiantefana whose field skills are enviable and enthusiasm appears limitless. As ever with book projects, Helen Gilkes and Tim Harris at Nature Picture Library have been supportive and allowed easy access to images. Nick is also grateful to Fixation in London, who efficiently service his Nikon camera equipment after the rigors of tropical travel have taken their toll.

FURTHER INFORMATION

Burrage, B. R., Comparative ecology and behaviour of *Chamaeleo pumilus pumilus* (Gmelin) and *C. namaquensis* A. Smith (Sauria: Chamaeleontidae), *Ann. S. Afr. Mus.* 61, 1973, 1–158.
Glaw, F. and Vences, M., *A Field Guide to the Amphibians and Reptiles of Madagascar*, Third edition. Cologne, Vences and Glaw Verlag, 2007, 496 pp.
Spawls, S., Howell,K., Drewes, R. and Ashe, J., *A Field Guide to the Reptiles of East Africa*. Academic Press, London and San Diego, 2002.
Tilbury, Colin, *Chameleons of Africa*. Edition Chimaira, Frankfurt am Main, 2010.
Tolley, K. and Burger, M., *Chameleons of Southern Africa*. Stuik, Cape Town, 2010.

WEBSITES

Uetz, P. et al., The Reptile Database www.reptile-database.org